Financial Astrology
Almanac
2015

M. G. BUCHOLTZ, B.Sc., MBA

Wood Dragon Books

Box 1216, Regina, Saskatchewan, Canada, S4P 3B4

www.wooddragonbooks.com

ISBN# 978-0-9685370-8-4

Financial Astrology Almanac 2015

Copyright 2014 Malcolm Bucholtz, B.Sc., MBA

Printed in Canada

CONTENTS

FIGURES

Financial Astrology Almanac 2015

ACKNOWLEDGMENTS

To my beautiful wife, Jeanne, who continues to inspire me in so many ways and without whose encouragement my published books would not have become reality.

Disclaimer

All material provided herein is based on material gleaned from mathematical and astrological publications researched by the author to supplement his own trading. This publication is written with sincere intent for those who actively trade and invest in the financial markets and who are looking to incorporate astrological phenomena and esoteric math into their market activity. While the material presented herein has proven reliable to the author in his personal trading and investing activity, there is no guarantee the material herein will continue to be reliable into the future. The author and publisher assume no liability whatsoever for any investment or trading decisions made by readers of this book. The reader alone is responsible for all trading and investment outcomes and is further advised not to exceed his or her risk tolerances when trading or investing on the financial markets.

Recommended Readings

The Bull, the Bear and the Planets, M.G. Bucholtz, (iUniverse, USA, 2013)

The Lost Science, M.G. Bucholtz, (iUniverse, USA, 2013)

The Universal Clock, J. Long, (P.A.S. Publishing, USA,)

McWhirter Theory of Stock Market Forecasting, L. McWhirter, (Astro Book Company, USA, 1938)

The Universe Within, N. Turok, (House of Anansi Press, Canada, 2012)

A Theory of Continuous Planet Interaction, Tony Waterfall, NCGR Research Journal, Volume 4, Spring 2014, pp67-87.

INTRODUCTION

Many market analysts and financial media commentators think daily news, quarterly earnings reports and corporate events drive stock prices.

I disagree.

The financial markets are a reflection of the mass psychological emotion of traders, investors and fund managers. The term *reflection* may even be too mild of a descriptor. It may be more accurate to boldly state that human emotion drives buying and selling decisions in the financial markets. When market participants are feeling positive, they are driven to buy. When they are feeling uncertain or negative, they are driven to sell.

Probing this idea deeper immediately yields the complex question - what drives human emotion?

Medical researchers still have not definitively answered this question. Some say changes in blood alkalinity or acidity impact our emotions. Some say changes in chemical hormones in the bloodstream are the cause. My humble opinion on this complex matter is that the ever-changing configurations of orbiting planets and other celestial bodies in our cosmos influence our body chemistry and thereby drive human emotion.

This opinion has been shaped by the many Astrology publications I have read over the past several years. A particularly insightful article authored by astrologer Tony Waterfall appeared recently in the Spring 2014 NCGR Research Journal. In this article Waterfall reminds readers that the Sun is the centre of our planetary system. The Sun emits massive amounts of solar radiation in all directions into the vastness of space. This radiation is called *solar wind*. This solar wind interacts with the magnetic fields around Mercury, Venus, Moon, Mars, Jupiter, Saturn, Uranus, Neptune and Pluto. These planets accept and then disburse the solar wind radiation. As the radiation is disbursed, a goodly amount of it finds its way towards the magnetic field around planet Earth. Changes in the density and speed of solar wind mean that the amount of radiation reaching Earth's magnetic field on a daily, weekly or monthly basis will be ever-changing. As a result, the intensity or flux of the Earth's magnetic field is also constantly changing. The alignment of the orbiting planets in our cosmos will also play a role in determining how much solar radiation is deflected towards Earth's magnetic field. A simplistic way of viewing this entire arrangement is to think of a billiards table as the cosmos. The various balls on the table are the planets and other celestial bodies. The solar radiation is the white cue ball bouncing and deflecting off other balls on the table. The human body is largely comprised of water. We all have an electrical field that runs through our tissues. Hence, basic physics demands that changes to the Earth's magnetic field will then induce subtle changes to our bodily electrical circuitry. These subtle changes, in my opinion, are what drive our emotional responses. But there is so much more to be understood. Scientists and psychologists who are on a quest to learn more have come to call the developing science of how the cosmos affects humans *cosmo-biology*.

Ancient civilizations as far back as the Babylonians too recognized cosmo-biology, but in a more rudimentary form. Their high priests tracked and recorded changes in the emotions of the people. These diviners and seers tracked events, both fortuitous and disastrous. Although they lacked the ability to comprehend the physics of solar wind and magnetic fields, they were able to visually spot planets Mercury, Venus, Mars, Jupiter and Saturn in the heavens. They correlated changes in human emotion and changes in societal events to these planets. They assigned to these planets the names of the various Deities revered by the people. They further identified and named various star constellations in the heavens and further divided the heavens into twelve signs. This was the birth of Astrology as we know it today.

Starting in the early 1900's, esoteric thinkers such as the famous Wall Street trader W.D. Gann noted that basic Astrology bore a striking correlation to changes on the financial markets. This was the birth of financial Astrology. Gann based his writings and forecasts on the synodic cycles between various planets. Gann also delved deep into esoteric math, notably square root math. He is well remembered for Gann Lines – a technique based on square roots. But Gann lived in a challenging time.

Statute laws in places like New York expressly forbade the use of occult science in business ventures. Gann therefore carefully concealed the basis for his market forecasts. Today many traders and investors try to emulate Gann but they do so in a linear fashion. What they are missing is the Astrology component, which is anything but linear.

In the 1930s, Louise McWhirter followed closely in Gann's footsteps. She identified an 18.6 year cyclical correlation between the general state of the American economy and the position of the North Node of Moon. Her methodology also extended to include the Moon passing by key points of the natal birth horoscope of the New York Stock Exchange. As well, she identified a correlation between price movement of a stock and those times when transiting Sun, Mars, Jupiter and Saturn made hard aspects to the natal Sun position in the stock's natal birth horoscope. But even McWhirter has an air of mystery about her. In my opinion, there was no such person as Louise McWhirter. I believe this name to be an alias for someone, perhaps well known on Wall Street, who had to protect his identity.

The late 1940s saw even further advancement in the field of financial Astrology when astrologer Garth Allen (a.k.a. Donald Bradley) produced his Siderograph Model. This complex model is based on aspects between the various transiting planets. Each aspect as it occurs is given a sinusoidal weighting as the *orb* between the planets varies. This model is as powerful today as it was in the late 1940s.

I personally began to embrace financial Astrology in 2012 which was a monumental shift given that my educational background comprises an Engineering degree and an MBA degree. Two linear-thinking, left brain degrees to be sure. Since 2012, my research and back-testing has satisfied me that a correlation does indeed exist between Astrology and the financial markets. This Almanac represents my fifth publication on the subject of financial Astrology.

This Almanac begins by offering you a fairly thorough look at the science of Astrology. What then follows is an examination of the New York Stock Exchange for the twelve months of calendar year 2015. Each monthly examination presents a summation of key dates when Astrology events stand a high probability of influencing human emotion. A look at various commodity futures and the astro phenomena that influence them then follows. Finally, I provide a look at Gann Lines and Harmonics, two esoteric mathematical concepts that should be used when applying Astrology to make trading and investing decisions.

I sincerely hope after you have applied the material in this Almanac to your trading and investing activity, you will embrace financial Astrology as a valuable tool. I further hope that you will frequently pause to reflect on the deeper connection between the financial markets and the emotions of mankind.

To further set the tone for what you are about to read in this Almanac, I present to you the following quotes on the subject of Astrology:

"An unfailing experience of mundane events in harmony with the changes occurring in the heavens, has instructed and compelled my unwilling belief." (Johannes Kepler – astronomer, mathematician 1571-1630)

"Heaven sends down its good and evil symbols and wise men act accordingly." (Confucius – Chinese philosopher 551-479 BC)

"The controls of life are structured as forms and nuclear arrangements, in relation with the motions of the universe." (Louis Pasteur-scientist 1822-1895)

"Oh the wonderful knowledge to be found in the stars. Even the smallest things are written there...if you had but skill to read." (Ben Franklin-one of the Founding Fathers of America 1706-1790)

"It's common knowledge that a large percentage of Wall Street brokers use Astrology." (Donald Reagan, formerly Ronald Reagan's Chief of Staff)

1. Mundane Astrology

Astrology is an ancient science focused on the correlation between the planets, events of nature and behaviour of mankind. This ancient science is rooted in thousands of years of observation across many civilizations.

- The ancient Sumerians, Akkadians and Babylonians between the 4th and 2nd centuries BC believed the affairs of mankind could be gauged by watching the motions of certain stars and planets. They recorded their predictions and future indications of prosperity and calamity on clay tablets. These early recordings form the foundation of modern day Astrology.
- Ancient Egyptian artifacts show that high priests Petosiris and Necepso who lived during the reign of Ramses II were revered for their knowledge of Astrology. The Egyptian culture is thought to have developed a 12 month x 30 day time keeping method based on the repeated appearances of constellations.
- Ancient Indian and Chinese artifacts reveal that Astrology held an esteemed place in those societies for many thousands of years.
- Hipparchus, Pythagoras and Plato are key names from the Greek era. Historians think Pythagoras assigned mathematical values to the relations between celestial bodies. Plato is thought to have offered up predictions relating celestial bodies to human fates. Hipparchus is thought to have compiled a star catalogue which popularized Astrology.
- In the latter years of the Roman empire, Astrology was used for political gain. Important military figures surrounded themselves with philosophers such as Ptolemy and Valens. In 126 AD, Ptolemy penned four books describing the influence of the stars. His works are collectively called the *Tetrabiblos*. In 160 AD, Valens penned *Anthologies* in which he further summarized the principles of Astrology.

Following the conversion of Emperor Constantine to Christianity in 312 AD, using Astrology for gain became a crime according to the Church of Rome. Astrology then began a slow retreat to the sidelines where for the most part it remains today. Despite Astrology's sidelining by a Church seeking to protect its authority, Astrology was still used by leading thinkers such as Galileo, Brahe, Nostradamus, Kepler, Bacon and Newton. Thanks to the tenacity of these men, Astrology was prevented from fading away altogether into a distant memory.

The Zodiac

The Sun is at the center of our solar system. The Earth, Moon, planets and various other asteroid bodies complete our planetary system. The various planets and other asteroid bodies rotate 360 degrees around the Sun following a path called the *ecliptic plane* as shown in Figure 1. Earth is slightly tilted (approximately 23 degrees) relative to the ecliptic plane. Projecting the Earth's equator into space produces the *celestial equator plane.* There are two points of intersection between the ecliptic plane and celestial equator plane. These points are commonly called the *vernal equinox* (occurring at March 20th) and the *autumnal equinox (occurring at September 20th)*. Dividing the ecliptic plane into twelve equal sections of 30 degrees results in what astrologers call the *zodiac*. The twelve portions of the zodiac have names including Aries, Cancer, Leo and so on. If these names sound familiar, they should. You routinely see all twelve names in the daily horoscope section of your morning newspaper. Figure 2 illustrates a *zodiac wheel.* The starting point or zero degree point of the zodiac wheel is the sign Aries, located at the vernal equinox of each year.

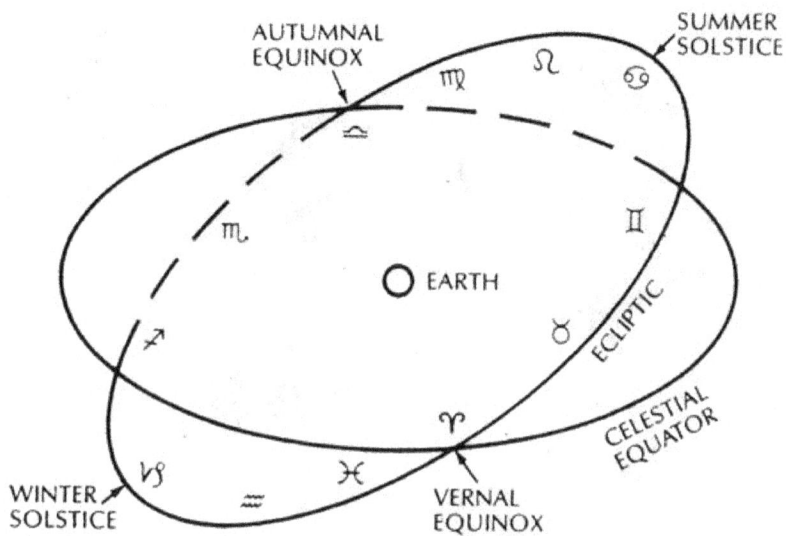

Figure 1 The Ecliptic

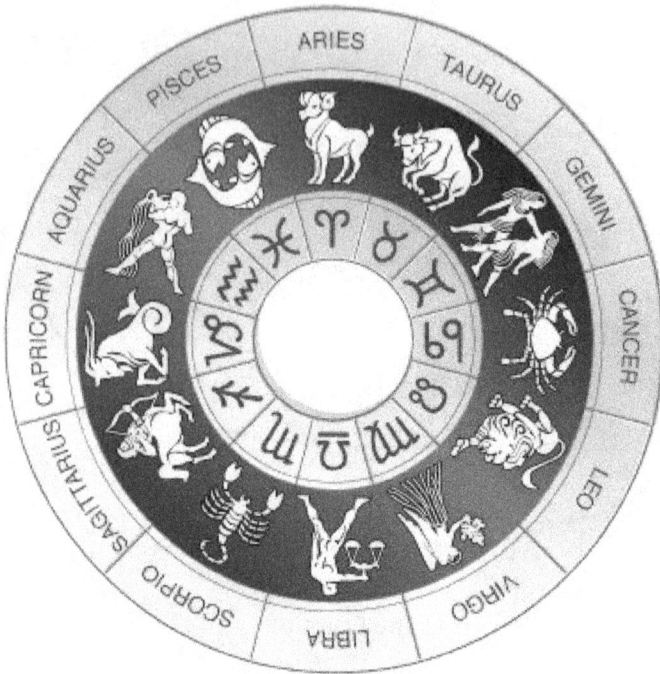

Figure 2 The Zodiac Wheel

If you have ever wondered about the names of the zodiac wheel portions, the following descriptions may be of interest. To ancient civilizations, each of these twelve signs was named after groupings and patterns of stars visible in the heavens to the high priests.

Aries (The Ram)

(0 to 30 degrees) 21 March – 20 April

According to Greek mythology, Nephele, the mother of Phrixus and Helle, gave her sons a ram with a golden fleece. To escape their evil stepmother, Hera, the sons mounted the ram and fled. When they reached the sea, Helles fell into the water and perished. Phrixus survived the ordeal and upon arriving in Colchis was received by King Aeetes who sacrificed the ram and dedicated the fleece to Zeus. Zeus then transported the ram into the heavens and made it into a constellation.

Taurus (The Bull)

(30 to 60 degrees) 21 April – 21 May

According to Roman legend, Jupiter took the form of a bull and became infatuated with the fair maiden Europa. When Europa decided to ride the bull, it rushed into the sea and whisked Europa off to Crete. Jupiter then raised the bull into the heavens where it became a star.

Gemini (The Twins)

(60 to 90 degrees) 22 May – 21 June

In Greek mythology, Hercules and Apollo are twins. In Roman legend, these twins are said to be Castor and Pollux, the sons of Leda. Pollux was the son of Zeus, who seduced Leda, while Castor was the son of Tyndareus, King of Sparta. Castor and Pollux are mythologically associated with St. Elmo's fire in their role as protectors of sailors. When Castor died, because he was mortal, Pollux begged Zeus to give Castor immortality. Zeus granted the wish by uniting Castor and Pollux together in the heavens as a constellation.

Cancer (The Crab)

(90 to 120 degrees) 22 June-23 July

Roman legend says that Cancer is the crab that bit Hercules during his fight with the Hydra monster. The crab was then placed in the heavens as a star by Juno, the enemy of Hercules.

Leo (The Lion)

(120 to 150 degrees) 24 July – 23 August

Legend says that Hercules battled with the Nemean lion and won. Zeus raised the lion to the heavens as a star.

Virgo (The Virgin)

(150 to 180 degrees) 24 August – 23 September

Legend has it that Virgo is a constellation modelled after Justitia, daughter of Astraeus and Ancora. Justitia lived before mankind sinned. After mankind sinned, Justitia returned to the heavens.

Libra (The Scales)

(180 to 210 degrees) 24 September – 23 October

Libra was known in Babylonian astronomy as a set of scales that were held sacred to the Sun God Shamash, the patron of truth and justice. In Roman mythology, Libra is considered to depict the scales held by Astraea , the Goddess of Justice.

Scorpio (The Scorpion)

(210 to 240 degrees) 24 October – 22 November

According to Greek mythology, Orion boasted to Diana and Latona that he could kill every animal on Earth. The ladies sent for a scorpion which stung Orion to death. Jupiter then raised the scorpion to the heavens as a constellation.

Sagittarius (The Archer)

(240 to 270 degrees) 23 November – 22 December

In Babylonian legend, Sagittarius was the God of War. In Greek legend, Sagittarius was a centaur (half man, half horse) in the act of shooting an arrow. In Roman legend, Sagittarius was a centaur who killed himself when he accidently dropped one of Hercules' poisoned arrows on his hoof.

Capricorn (The Goat)

(270 to 300 degrees) 23 December – 20 January

In Greek legend, during the war with the giants the Greek Gods were driven into Egypt. In order to escape the wrath of the encroaching giants, each Greek God changed his shape. The God Pan leapt into the river Nile and turned the upper part of his body into a goat and the lower part into a fish. This combination was deemed worthy by Jupiter who raised Pan to the heavens.

Aquarius (The Water Bearer)

(300 to 330 degrees) 21 January – 19 February

According to legend, Deucalion- the son of Prometheus, was raised to the heavens after surviving the great deluge that flooded the world.

Pisces (The Fishes)

(330 to 360 degrees) 20 February - 20 March

In Greek legend, Aphrodite and Eros were surprised by Typhon while playing along the river Nile. To escape, they jumped into the water and were changed into two fishes.

2. Financial Astrology

The Celestial Bodies

In addition to the Sun and Moon, there are eight celestial bodies important to the application of Astrology to trading and investing on the financial markets. These planets are Mercury, Venus, Mars, Jupiter, Saturn, Uranus, Neptune and Pluto.

The Glyphs

These planets and the twelve signs of the zodiac are denoted by strange looking symbols, called *glyphs*. Figure 3 presents the glyphs.

Points		Zodiac Signs	
☉	Sun	♈	Aries
☽	Moon	♉	Taurus
☿	Mercury	♊	Gemini
♀	Venus	♋	Cancer
♂	Mars	♌	Leo
♃	Jupiter	♍	Virgo
♄	Saturn	♎	Libra
♅	Uranus	♏	Scorpio
♆	Neptune	♐	Sagittarius
♇ ♇	Pluto	♑	Capricorn
		♒	Aquarius
		♓	Pisces

Figure 3 – The Glyphs

Ascendant, Descendant, MC and IC

As the Earth rotates on its axis once in every 24 hours, an observer situated on Earth will detect an apparent motion of the zodiac. To better define this motion, astrologers apply four cardinal points to the zodiac, almost like the north, south, east and west points on a compass. These cardinal points divide the zodiac into four quadrants. The east point is termed the *Ascendant* and is often abbreviated Asc. The west point is termed the *Descendant* and is often abbreviated Dsc. The south point is termed the *Mid-Heaven* (from the Latin *Medium Coeli*) and is often abbreviated MC. The north point is termed the *Imum Coeli* (Latin for bottom of the sky) and is abbreviated IC.

Geocentric and Heliocentric Astrology

Financial Astrology comes in two distinct varieties – *geocentric* and *heliocentric*.

In *geocentric* Astrology, the Earth is the vantage point for observing the planets as they pass through the signs of the zodiac. Owing to the different times for the planets to each orbit the Sun, an astrologer situated on Earth would see the planets making distinct angles (called *aspects*) with one another and also with the Sun. The aspects that are commonly used in Astrology are 0, 30, 45, 60, 90, 120, 150 and 180 degrees. In Financial Astrology, it is common to refer to only the 0, 45, 90, 120 and 180 degree aspects.

In *heliocentric* Astrology, the Sun is the vantage point for observing the planets as they pass through the signs of the zodiac. An observer positioned on the Sun would also see the orbiting planets making *aspects* with one another.

To identify these aspects, astrologers use Ephemeris Tables. For geocentric Astrology, the *New American Ephemeris for the 21ˢᵗ Century* is commonly used. It is available at most bookstores. For heliocentric Astrology, the *American Heliocentric Ephemeris* is a good resource. It tends to be harder to find in bookstores but on-line booksellers may have it available.

For faster aspect determination, two excellent software programs available are *Millenium Trax* produced by AIR Software and *Solar Fire Gold* produced by Astrolabe.

Lunar Astrology

On any clear night the Moon will be visible in one of its various phases. The Moon is the closest of all the planetary bodies to the Earth and has long been held in fascination by mankind.

Throughout the centuries, the Moon has been associated with health, mood and dreams. In 6th century Constantinople (modern day Istanbul, Turkey), physicians at the court of Emperor Justinian advised that gout could be cured by inscribing verses of Homer on a copper plate when the Moon was in the sign of Libra or Leo. In 17th century France, astrologers used the Moon to explain mood changes in women. In 17th century England, herbal remedy practitioners advised people to pluck the petals of the peony flower when the Moon was waning. During the Renaissance period, it was thought that dreams could come true if the Moon was in the signs of Taurus, Leo, Aquarius or Scorpio.

Today, such ideas about the Moon are no more. But, the Moon nonetheless continues to be recognized as a powerful celestial body. Just as the gravitational pull of the Moon can influence the action of ocean tides, this same pull somehow also influences our emotions of fear and hope. As our emotions of fear and hope change, our investment buying and selling decisions also change. These emotional changes correlate to changes in price trend action. When this correlation is overlaid with technical chart analysis, a whole new dimension in trading and investing opens up.

The Lunar Month

Just as the planets orbit 360 degrees around the Sun, the Moon orbits 360 degrees around the Earth. The Moon orbits the Earth in a plane of motion called the *lunar orbit plane*. This plane is inclined at about 5 degrees to the celestial equator plane of the Earth. The Moon orbits Earth with a slightly elliptical pattern in approximately 27.3 days, relative to an observer located on a fixed frame of reference such as the Sun. This time period is known as a *sidereal month*. However, during one sidereal month, an observer located on Earth (a moving frame of reference) will revolve part way around the Sun. To that Earth-bound observer, a complete orbit of the Moon around the Earth will appear longer than the sidereal month at approximately 29.5 days. This 29.5 day period of time is known as a *synodic month* or more commonly a *lunar month*.

Retrograde and Elongation

The planet Earth advances about 1 degree per day in its orbit around the Sun. Mercury advances about 4 degrees per day. To an observer stationed on the Sun, the orbiting planets will appear much like race cars on a track going around and around the Sun.

There will be three or four times during a year when Earth and Mercury pass by each other on this celestial racetrack. There will be one or perhaps two times per year when Earth and Venus pass each other. There will be one time every two years when Earth and Mars pass each other.

To an observer positioned on Earth, an optical illusion occurs on this celestial racetrack. As Mercury, Venus or Mars passes by Earth, it appears as through these planets are briefly not moving in the heavens. These brief illusory periods are what astrologers call Retrograde events. To ancient societies, Retrograde events were of great significance as human emotion was often seen to be changeable at these events.

For 2015, Mercury will be Retrograde from:

January 22 through February 10
May 19 through June 11
September 18 through October 9

For 2015, Venus will be Retrograde from July 25 through September 5.

Mars will not have any Retrograde events in 2015.

Mercury orbits the Sun in about 88 days. Its orbit is not circular, but rather slightly elliptical. There will be times when Mercury is far from the Sun and there will be times when it is close to the Sun. These events are what astronomers call Elongation events. Elongation events are closely related to Retrograde events in that elongation maxima occur on either side of Retrograde events. Both Elongation and Retrograde events can be seen to play a role in human emotion and changes on the financial markets.

For 2015, Mercury will experience elongation maxima on January 14 and February 24, again on May 7 and June 24, again on September 4 and October 16 and finally on December 29.

Declination

Declination refers to the positioning of a planet above or below the Earth's celestial equator plane. My back-testing research has revealed that somehow changes in the declination of a planet affect the human psyche. Planets experience declinations of up to about 25 degrees above and below the celestial equator plane.

Mercury, Venus, Mars and indeed Earth itself endure frequent changes in declination due to the gravitational force of the Sun. Planets like Jupiter, Saturn, Neptune, Uranus and Pluto also experience declination changes but these changes are slow to evolve.

What follows is a monthly summation of when to expect declination changes in 2015.

Mercury

In December 2014, Mercury will be at about -25 degrees declination. From this low point, Mercury will begin to climb higher in declination.

Between January 20 and February 1, Mercury will make an inflection point in its declination path.

Between February 10 and 28th, Mercury will again exhibit an inflection in its declination.

Between April 1 and 4th, Mercury will pass through the 0 degree level of declination.

Between May 3 and 19th, Mercury will be at about 25 degrees declination – its highest point for 2015.

As Mercury begins to slowly fall in declination, it will make an inflection between June 4 and 23rd.

Between July 7th and 21st, Mercury will again exhibit an inflection point.

Between August 23rd and 27th, Mercury will pass through 0 degrees of declination.

Between September 13 and 22nd, Mercury will make an inflection point again.

Between October 6 and 17th, Mercury will make another inflection – this one very close to 0 degrees of declination.

Between December 3 and 21, Mercury will reach its lowest declination level for 2015.

Figure 4 presents a plot of Mercury declination for 2014 and 2015.

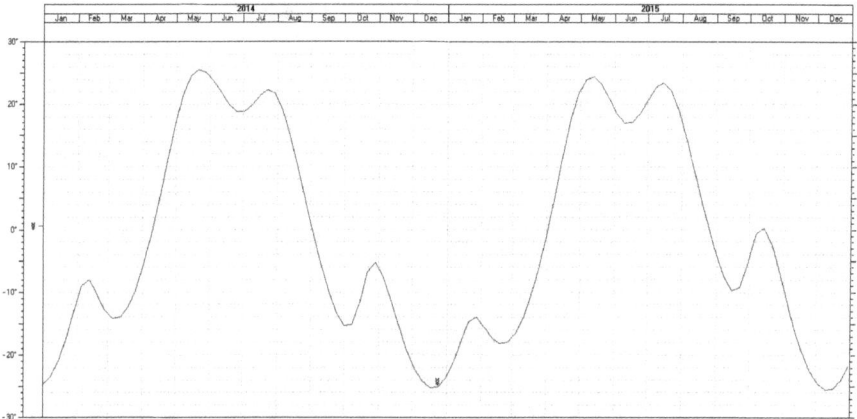

Figure 4 – Mercury Declination Path 2014-2015

Venus

In December 2014, Venus recorded a declination low at -24 degrees. From February 17-26th, it will cross over the 0 degrees of declination point. Between April 28th and May 25th, Venus will record its declination maximum for 2015 at 26 degrees.

Following this maximum, Venus will slowly decline in its declination. From July 28 to August 21, Venus will record an inflection. Another inflection will come between September 6 and October 6.

Between November 6 and 14th, Venus will cross through 0 degrees of declination on its way to a declination minimum in early 2016.

Figure 5 presents a plot of Venus declination for 2014 and 2015.

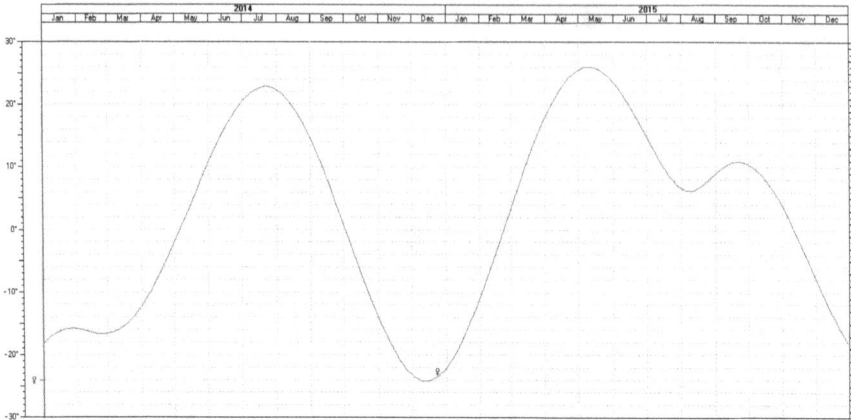

Figure 5– Venus Declination Path 2014-2015

Mars

In late October 2014, Mars recorded its declination low.

Between February 17 and 26th, Mars will pass through 0 degrees of declination.

Between June 2 and July 21, Mars will record its maximum declination for 2015.

Between November 14 and 23, Mars will pass through 0 degrees of declination.

Figure 6 presents a plot of Mars declination for 2014 and 2015.

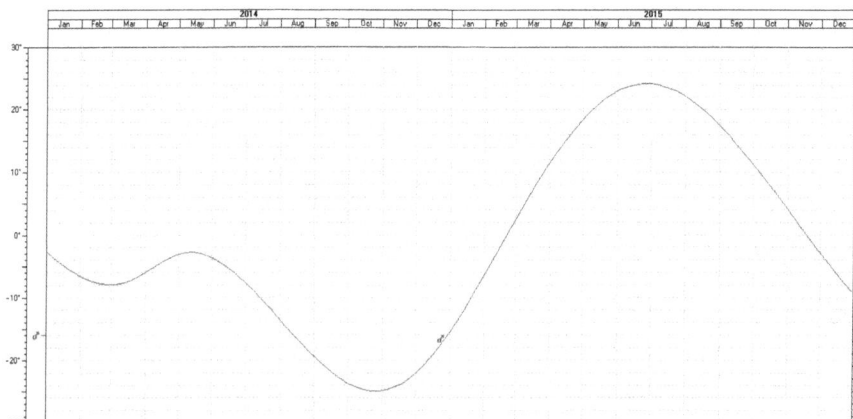

Figure 6 – Mars Declination Path 2014-2015

Sun

Declination of Sun really does not ever change. What does change is how we on Earth view the Sun.

From March 18 to 23, the Sun from our viewpoint on Earth passes through 0 degrees of declination. This point in our calendar year has come to be called the Spring Equinox.

From June 3 to July 8, the Sun passes through its declination maximum for the year. This is what is commonly called the Summer Solstice.

From September 20 to 26, Sun passes through 0 degrees declination. This is what is commonly called the Autumn Equinox.

From December 9 to 30, Sun passes through its lowest declination level for the year. This is what is commonly referred to as the Winter Solstice.

Figure 7 presents a plot of Sun declination for 2014 and 2015.

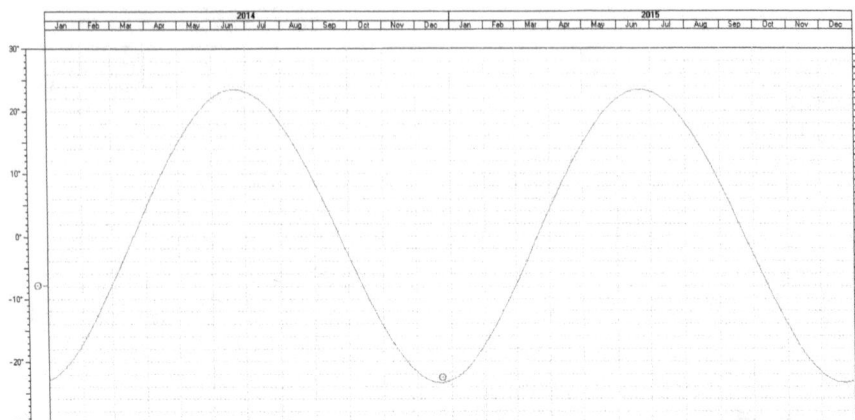

Figure 7 – Sun Declination Path 2014-2015

Moon

During each lunar cycle, the Moon can be seen to vary in its position above and below the lunar ecliptic.

Figure 8 presents a plot of Moon declination for 2015.

Take a look at a daily chart of a stock you like to trade or invest in. Take a look at a commodity futures contract you follow. You will very likely find that at times of maximum or minimum lunar declination there will be a change in price behavior best witnessed on an hourly chart.

To assist you in some back-testing of your own, consider that in 2014, Moon recorded maximums in declination on January 13, February 9, March 9, April 5, May 2, May 30, June 26, July 23. August 20, September 16, October 14, November 10, December 7.

To further assist you, consider that in 2014, Moon recorded minimums in declination on January 28, February 24, March 23, April 19 May 16, June 13, July 10, August 6, September 3, September 30, October 27, November 24, December 21.

For 2015, Moon will record maximums in its declination on January 3, January 31, February 27, March 26, April 23, May 20, June 17, July 14, August 10, September 6, October 4, October 31, November 27 and

December 26.

For 2015, Moon will record minimums in its declination on January 18, February 15, March 14, April 11, May 7, June 4, July 1, July 28, August 25, September 22, October 19, November 15 and December 11.

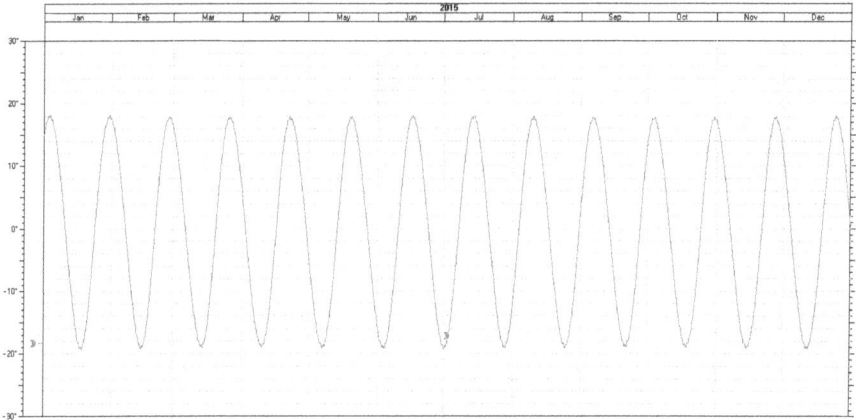

Figure 8 – Moon Declination Path 2015

3. New York Stock Exchange

2015 Astrology

The Lunation and the New York Stock Exchange

A *lunation* is the astrological term for a New Moon. At a lunation, the Sun and Moon are separated by 0 degrees which means the Sun and Moon are together in the same sign of the zodiac. The correlation between the monthly lunation event and New York Stock Exchange price movements was first popularized in 1937 by trader Louise McWhirter. In her book, *Theory of Stock Market Forecasting*, she discussed how lunations making hard aspects to planets such as Mars, Jupiter, Saturn and Uranus were indicative of coming volatility on the New York Stock Exchange. She also paid close attention to Mars and Neptune - the two planets that *rule* the New York Stock Exchange. McWhirter said those times of a lunar month when the transiting Moon makes 0 degree aspects to Mars and Neptune should be watched carefully.

New York Stock Exchange – First Trade Chart

The New York Stock Exchange officially opened for business on May 17, 1792. As the following chart shows, The NYSE has its Ascendant (Asc) at 14 degrees Cancer and its Mid-Heaven (MC) at 24 Pisces.

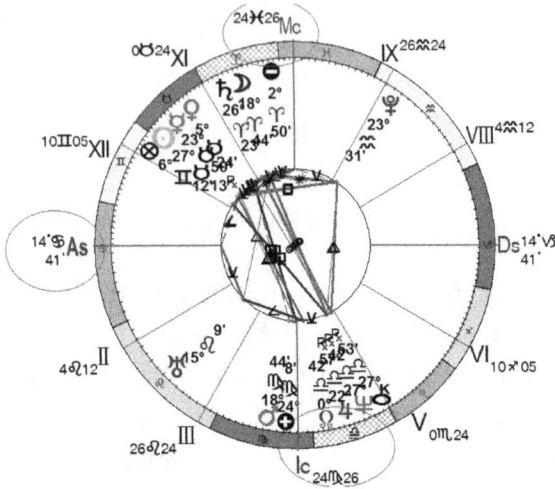

NYSE natal chart
May 17, 1792
7:52 am

Figure 9: NYSE First Trade Chart

McWhirter further paid close attention to those times in the monthly lunar cycle when the transiting Moon passed by the NYSE natal Asc and MC locations at 14 Cancer and 24 Pisces respectively.

Horoscope Charts and the McWhirter Methodology

In my research and writing, I follow the McWhirter methodology. When forecasting whether or not a coming month will be volatile or not for the NYSE, the McWhirter methodology starts with creating a horoscope chart for the New Moon date and positioning the Ascendant of the chart at 14 degrees Cancer - which is the Ascendant position on the 1792 natal chart of the New York Stock Exchange. Aspects to the lunation are then studied and planets that happen to be in the 10th House are also noted.

Similarly, when studying an individual stock or an individual commodity futures contract, the McWhirter approach calls for the creation of a horoscope chart at the First Trade date of the stock or commodity. The Ascendant is then shifted so that the Sun is at the Ascendant.

In stock and commodity analyses, McWhirter then paid strict attention to those times of a calendar year when transiting Sun, Mars, Jupiter, Saturn,

Neptune and Uranus made hard 0,90 and 180 degree aspects to the natal Mid-Heaven, natal Ascendant, natal Sun, natal Jupiter and even the natal Moon of the individual stock or commodity future being studied.

What one must be alert for at these hard aspects is the possibility of a trend change, the possibility of increased volatility within a trend or even the possibility of a breakout from a chart consolidation pattern. Evidence of such changes will be found by watching price action relative to moving averages and oscillator type functions (MAC-D, DMI, RSI and so on). This Almanac assumes that the reader is reasonably well versed in chart technical analysis.

McWhirter Lunation Examples

The following three examples of the McWhirter method are taken from calendar year 2014. The months of January, February and June were significant for various reasons.

January 2014

The New Moon in January 2014 occurred on January 1 at 10 degrees Capricorn. The horoscope wheel in Figure 10 depicts planetary placements just prior to the New Moon with the Ascendant at 14 Cancer - the same location it was at in 1792 when the New York Stock exchange was formed.

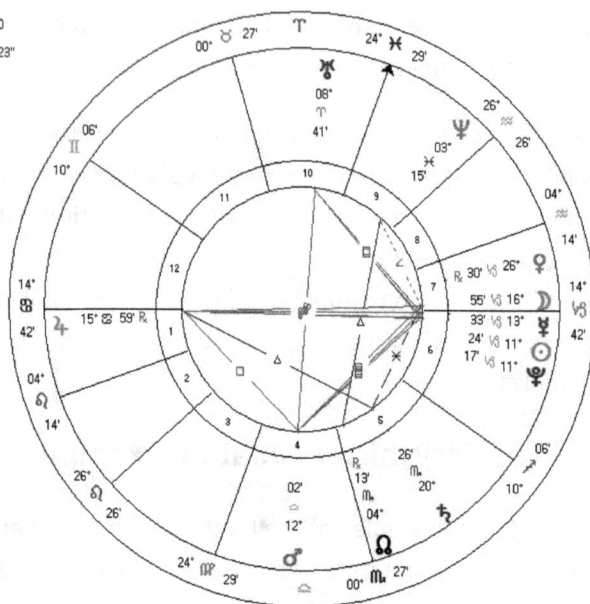

Figure 10 Lunation Event of January 1, 2014

Note that the lunation makes a hard 90 degree aspect to aggressive planet Mars and heavy-weight planet Uranus. Definitely two warning signs of volatility to come. And in fact, the month of January 2014 was a nasty one on the New York Stock Exchange with the S&P500 exhibiting a drop of just over 100 points.

February 2014

The next New Moon in 2014 occurred on January 30 at 11 degrees Aquarius. The horoscope wheel in Figure 11 depicts planetary placements just prior to the New Moon with the Ascendant at 14 Cancer.

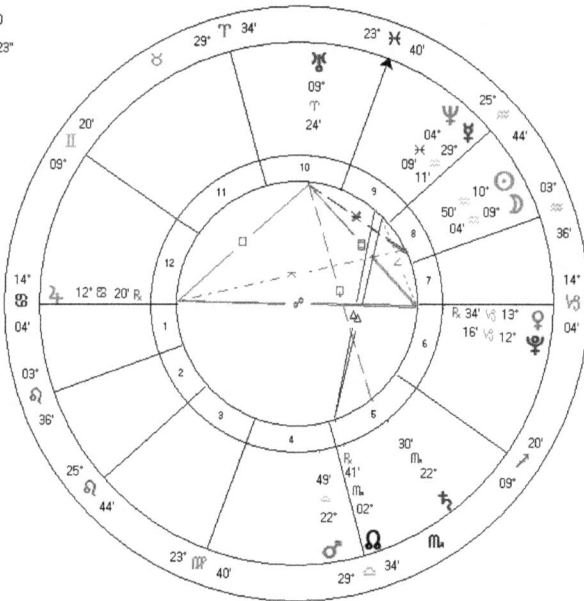

Figure 11 Lunation Event of January 30, 2014

Note that the lunation makes a soft 60 degree aspect to Uranus. No other aspects are apparent which bodes well for positive market performance. And in fact, the New York Stock Exchange made a bottom early in February and by month end the S&P500 had surpassed the January highs.

June 2014

The New Moon in June 2014 occurred on June 27 at 5 degrees Cancer –
just shy of the natal Asc position of the NYSE. The horoscope wheel in
Figure 12 depicts planetary placements just prior to the New Moon with
the Ascendant at 14 Cancer.

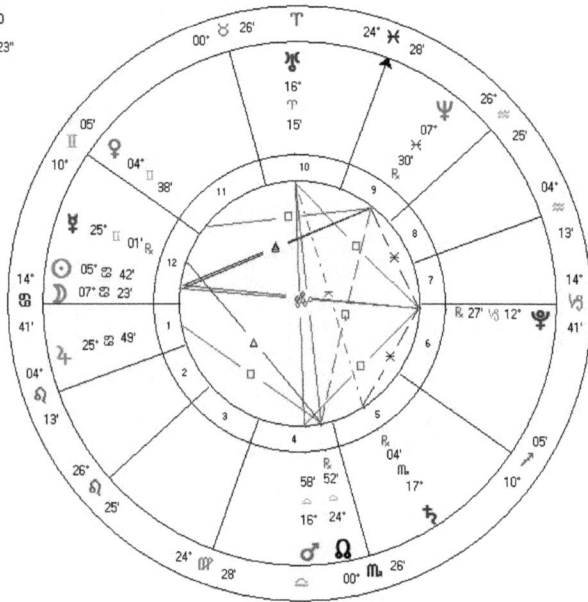

Figure 12 Lunation Event of June 27, 2014

Aside from being very close to the natal Asc location, the lunation also
makes a 120 degree aspect to Neptune, one of the co-rulers of the NYSE.
Having a lunation that touches two sensitive points of the NYSE certainly
demands close attention. And in fact, as transiting Moon passed by Mars
on July 7, the S&P500 recorded a record high. This record high was tested
on July 16 as Moon passed by Neptune, the other co-ruler of the NYSE.
Late on July 16 and into July 17, Moon passed over the natal MC position
of the NYSE. This sparked a violent price reaction with the S&P500
plunging 27 points as news of the downing of Malaysian Air flight MH17
over Ukraine crossed the newswires.

2015 Lunation Forecasts

December 2014

Key Dates

The New Moon in December 2014 occurs on the 21st with Sun at 0 degrees Capricorn. The horoscope in Figure 13 depicts planetary placements just hours prior to the New Moon with the Ascendant at 14 of Cancer.

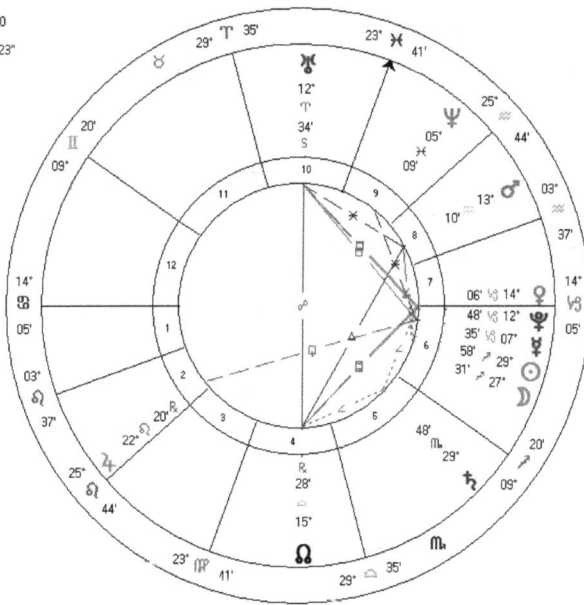

Event of 21 Dec 2014
Event Chart
21 Dec 2014, Sun
6:31:12 pm EDT +4:00
New York, NY
40°N42'51" 074°W00'23"
Geocentric
Tropical
Placidus
Mean Node
Parallax Moon

Figure 13 – New Moon December 21, 2014

The lunar cycle commencing at this New Moon will run until January 20, 2015. The lunation makes no hard aspects to any planets which is a positive indication for the coming lunar cycle.

Key dates to be alert to during this cycle include:

December 24: Moon transits past Mars. Watch for a reaction on what will be a shortened trading day ahead of the Holiday Season.

December 26: Moon transits past Neptune. The NYSE will most likely be closed so this transit matters not.

December 27: Moon transits past 24 Pisces (natal MC of NYSE). This date is a Saturday, so watch for a reaction on financial markets on the following Monday.

December 28: Moon transits past 10th House planet Uranus. This date is a Sunday. Watch for a market reaction on the Monday.

January 1-9: Sun transits 180 degrees to 14 Cancer (natal Asc of NYSE)

January 4: Moon transits past 14 Cancer (natal Asc of NYSE). This date is a Sunday, so watch for a reaction on the financial markets the next day, Monday.

January 5-14: Mars transits through 90 degrees to natal Sun

January 6-10: Sun transits 90 degrees to natal Moon

January 10-14: Sun transits 90 degrees natal Jupiter

January 2015

Key Dates

The New Moon in January occurs on the 20th with Sun at 0 degrees Aquarius. The horoscope in Figure 14 depicts planetary placements just hours prior to the New Moon as the Ascendant passes 14 Cancer.

The lunar cycle commencing at this New Moon will run until February 18, 2015. This lunation is interesting in that the two rulers of the New York Stock Exchange, Neptune and Mars are both conjunct at 5-6 degrees of Pisces. The lunation itself is a benign 30 degrees to these two planets. The lunation itself makes a favorable 60 degree aspect to Saturn. No hard aspects can be seen. The coming lunar cycle should be generally favorable for the NYSE.

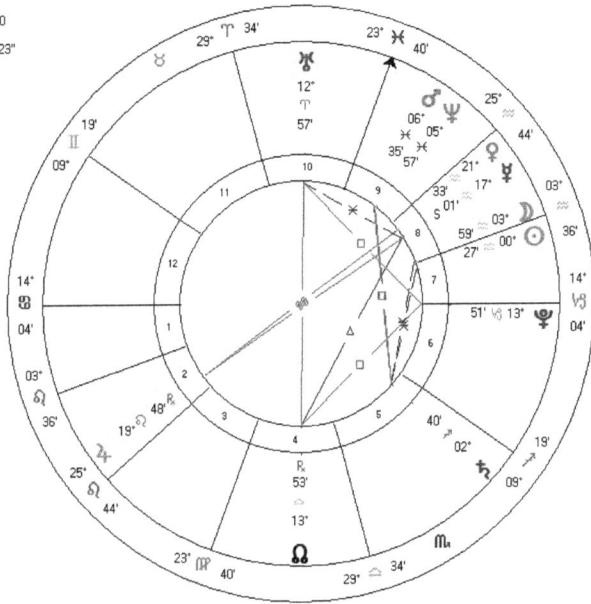

Event of 20 Jan 2015
Event Chart
20 Jan 2015, Tue
4:33:12 pm EDT +4:00
New York, NY
40°N42'51" 074°W00'23"
Geocentric
Tropical
Placidus
Mean Node
Parallax Moon

Figure 14 – New Moon January 20, 2015

Key dates to be alert to during this lunar cycle include:

January 22-23: Moon transits past Mars and Neptune and Moon transits the natal MC position at 24 Pisces.

February 1: Sun transits 14 Cancer , the natal Asc position of the New York Stock Exchange. This date is a Sunday. Watch for a market reaction when markets open on Monday.

February 1-11: Sun will transit through a 180 degree hard aspect to Jupiter. Such hard aspects have a strong tendency to align to changes of trend on the Dow Jones Industrial Average and S&P500.

February 7-18: Mars passes through a 0 degree aspect to the natal MC

February 13-18: Sun passes through a 90 degree aspect to natal Sun

February 2015

Key Dates

The New Moon in February occurs on the 18th with Sun at 29 degrees Aquarius. The following horoscope in Figure 15 depicts planetary placements just hours prior to the New Moon as the Ascendant passes 14 Cancer.

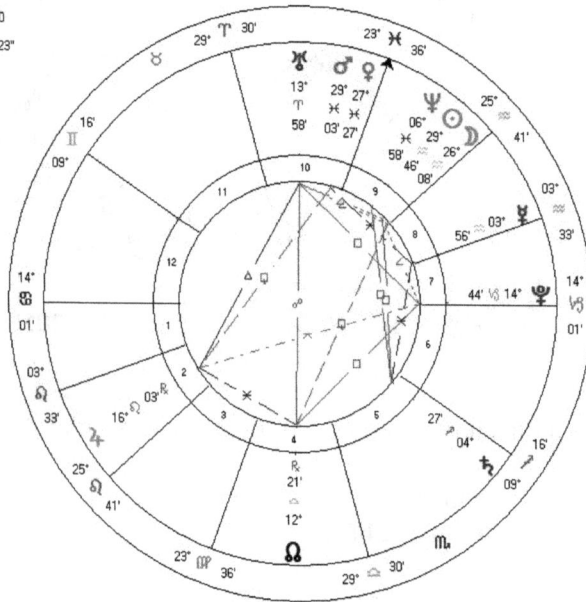

Figure 15 – New Moon February 18, 2015

The lunar cycle commencing at this New Moon will run until March 20, 2015. This lunation is interesting in that it makes a hard 90 degree aspect to heavy-weight planet Saturn. The lunation is also within orb of being conjunct to Neptune, one of the co-rulers of the New York Stock Exchange. The other co-ruler, Mars, is situated in the 10th House. This lunar cycle could be a challenging one on the NYSE.

Key dates to be alert to during this lunation include:

February 18-27: Sun will transit through a 90 degree hard aspect to Saturn. Such hard aspects have a strong tendency to align to changes of trend on the Dow Jones Industrial Average and S&P500.

February 19: Moon transits past Neptune.

February 20-21: Moon transits past 24 Pisces, the natal MC of the NYUSE. Moon also transits past co-ruler Mars on the 21st. This is a Saturday, so watch for a market reaction on the Friday.

February 28: Moon transits past 14 Cancer, the natal Asc of the NYSE. This is a Saturday, so watch for a market reaction on the Friday.

March 5-15: Mars transits through a 90 degree hard aspect to natal Asc

March 13-17: Sun transits through a 0 degree aspect to natal MC.

March 11-21: Mars transits past a 0 degree aspect to natal Moon

March 18: Moon transits past Neptune.

Note: On March 17-18 the Federal Reserve will conduct one of its Open Market Committee meetings which will conclude with Governor Yellen speaking to the media about monetary policy.

March 2015

Key Dates

The New Moon in March occurs on the 20th with Sun at 29 degrees Pisces. The following horoscope in Figure 16 depicts planetary placements just hours prior to the New Moon as the Ascendant passes 14 Cancer.

The lunar cycle commencing at this New Moon will run until April 18, 2015. The lunation is 120 degrees to Saturn. This lunation occurs within the 10th House along with Mars and Uranus and is also within orb of being conjunct to the natal MC of the NYSE. Watch for increased volatility on the NYSE in what could be another challenging month.

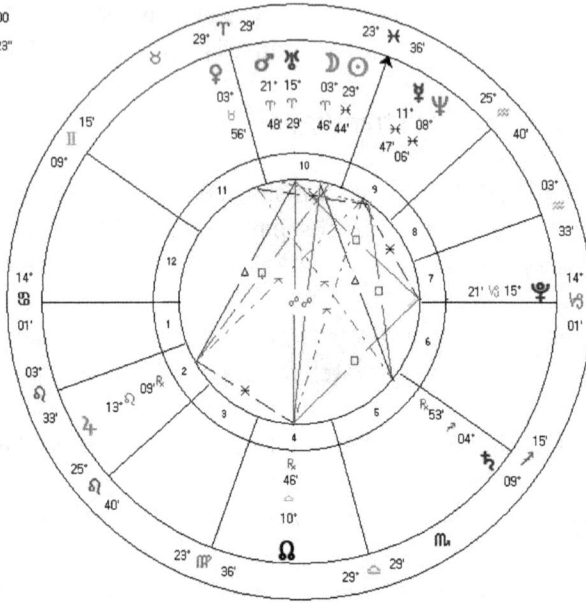

Figure 16 – New Moon March 20, 2015

Key dates to be alert to during this lunation include:

March 21: Moon transits past co-ruler Mars.

March 27: Moon transits past 14 Cancer, the natal Asc of the NYSE

April 2-6: Sun transits past a 90 degree aspect to natal Asc

April 6-10: Sun transits past a 0 degree aspect to natal Moon

April 15: Moon transits past co-ruler Neptune

April 2015

Key Dates

The New Moon in April occurs on the 18th with Sun at 28 degrees Aries. The horoscope in Figure 17 depicts planetary placements just hours prior to the New Moon as the Ascendant passes 14 Cancer.

The lunar cycle commencing at this New Moon will run until May 17, 2015. The lunation occurs in the 10th House and is 135 degrees to Pluto and 150 degrees to Saturn. The other hard aspect visible is a 45 degree aspect to Neptune.

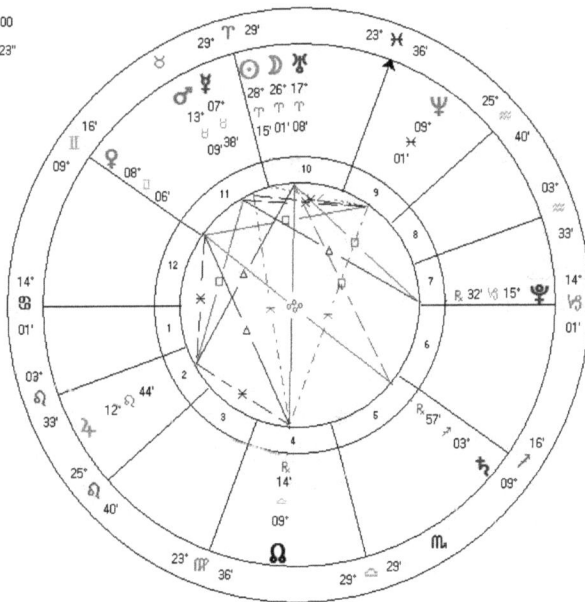

Figure 17 – New Moon April 18, 2015

Key dates to be alert to during this lunation include:

April 19: Moon transits past co-ruler Mars. This date is a Sunday, so watch for a possible market reaction on the Monday.

April 24: Moon transits past 14 Cancer, the natal Asc of the NYSE

April 29-May 9: Sun will transit through a 90 degree hard aspect to Jupiter. Such hard aspects have a strong tendency to align to changes of trend on the Dow Jones Industrial Average and S&P500.

Note: just as this Sun-Jupiter aspect gets underway, the Federal Reserve will be concluding one of its Open Market Committee meetings.

May 2-14: Mars transits past a 0 degree aspect to natal Sun

May 12: Moon transits past co-ruler Neptune.

May 13: Moon transits 24 Pisces, the natal MC position of the NYSE

May 2015

Key Dates

The New Moon in May occurs on the 17th with Sun at 26 degrees Taurus. The horoscope in Figure 18 depicts planetary placements several hours prior to the New Moon as the Ascendant passes 14 Cancer.

The lunar cycle commencing at this New Moon will run until June 16, 2015. The lunation is within orb of being conjunct to Mars. The lunation is also opposite Saturn. Watch for a trend change on the NYSE during this lunar cycle.

Event of 17 May 2015
Event Chart
17 May 2015, Sun
8:52:57 am EDT +4:00
New York, NY
40°N42'51" 074°W00'23"
Geocentric
Tropical
Placidus
Mean Node
Parallax Moon

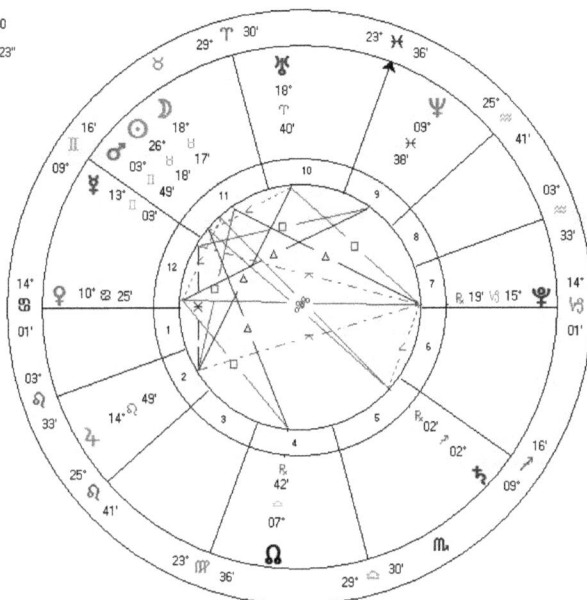

Figure 18 – New Moon May 17, 2015

Key dates to be alert to during this lunation include:

May 15-20: Sun transits past a 0 degree aspect to natal Sun

May 16-26: Sun will transit through a 180 degree hard aspect to Saturn. Such hard aspects have a strong tendency to align to changes of trend on the Dow Jones Industrial Average and S&P500.

May 18: Moon transits past co-ruler Mars.

May 21: Moon transits past 14 Cancer, the natal Asc of the NYSE

June 8: Moon transits past co-ruler Neptune.

June 9: Moon transits past 24 Pisces, the natal MC position of the NYSE

June 15: Sun is conjunct Mars

June 2015

Key Dates

The New Moon in June occurs on the 16th with Sun at 24 degrees Gemini. The following horoscope depicts planetary placements several hours prior to the New Moon as the Ascendant passes 14 Cancer.

The lunar cycle commencing at this New Moon will run until July 15, 2015. The lunation is conjunct Mars. No other hard aspects are visible.

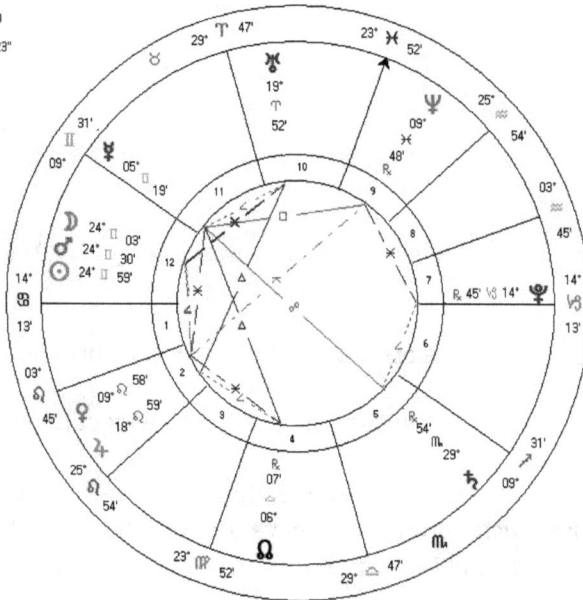

Figure 19 – New Moon June 16, 2015

Key dates to be alert to during this lunation include:

Note: On June 16-17 the Federal Reserve will conduct one of its Open Market Committee meetings which will conclude with Governor Yellen speaking to the media about monetary policy.

June 15-17: Sun passes through a 90 degree aspect to natal MC position of the NYSE.

June 17: Moon transits past 14 Cancer, the natal Asc of the NYSE

July 6-8: Sun transits 0 degrees to natal Asc

July 6: Moon transits past co-ruler Neptune.

July 7: Moon transits past 24 Pisces, the natal MC position of the NYSE

July 8-12: Sun transits 90 degrees to natal Moon

July 9-21: Mars transits past a 0 degree aspect to natal Asc

July 15: Moon transits past co-ruler Mars

July 2015

Key Dates

The New Moon in July occurs on the 15th with Sun at 22 degrees Cancer. The horoscope in Figure 20 depicts planetary placements several hours prior to the New Moon as the Ascendant passes 14 Cancer.

The lunar cycle commencing at this New Moon will run until August 14, 2015.

The lunation is 120 degrees to Saturn. More curious, however, is the location of Mars – right at the natal Ascendant position of the NYSE. This suggests either a significant trend shift on the NYSE or a marked increase in volatility.

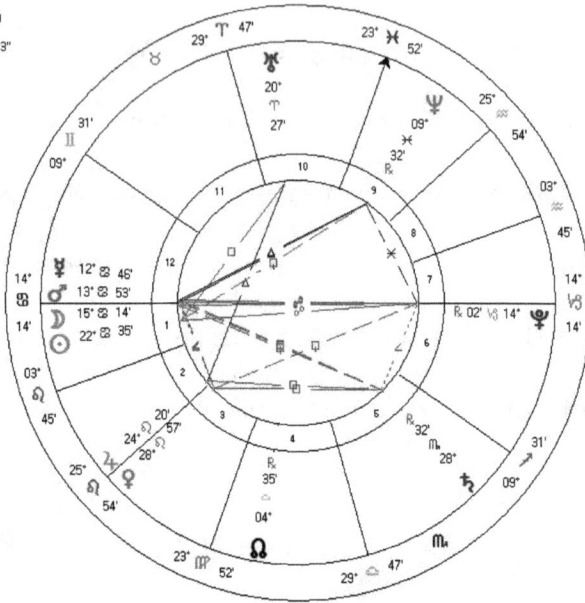

Event of 15 Jul 2015
Event Chart
15 Jul 2015, Wed
5:01:57 am EDT +4:00
New York, NY
40°N42'51" 074°W00'23"
Geocentric
Tropical
Placidus
Mean Node
Parallax Moon

Figure 20 – New Moon July 15, 2015

Key dates to be alert to during this lunation include:

July 13-17: Sun passes 90 degrees to natal Jupiter

July 15-28: Mars transits 90 degrees to natal Moon

July 21-August 4: Mars transits 90 degrees natal Jupiter

August 2-3: Moon transits past co-ruler Neptune and the natal MC position at 24 Pisces

August 11: Moon transits past 14 Cancer

August 12: Moon transits past co-ruler Mars

August 2015

Key Dates

The New Moon in August occurs on the 14th with Sun at 21 degrees Leo. The horoscope in Figure 21 depicts planetary placements several hours prior to the New Moon as the Ascendant passes 14 Cancer.

The lunation can be seen to be 120 degrees to heavy-weight planet Uranus and very nearly 90 degrees hard aspect to heavy-weight planet Saturn.

The lunar cycle commencing at this New Moon will run until September 13, 2015.

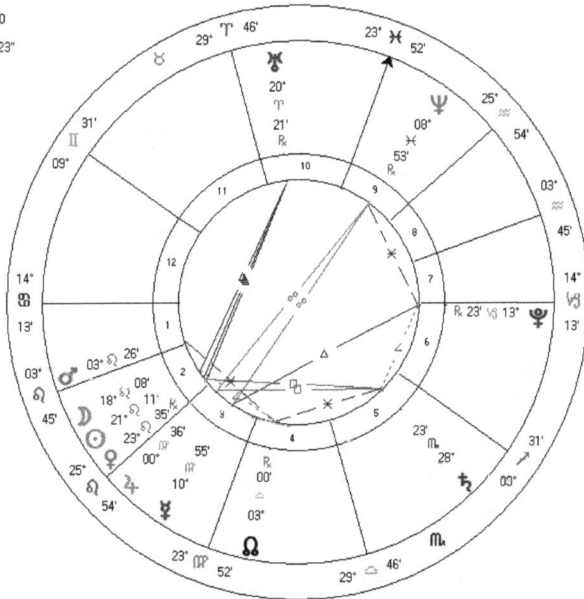

Figure 21 – New Moon August 14, 2015

Key dates to be alert to during this lunation include:

August 16-September 3: Sun will transit through a 0 degree hard aspect to Jupiter and also a 90 degree hard aspect to Saturn. Such hard aspects have a strong tendency to align to changes f trend on the Dow Jones Industrial Average and S&P500.

August 18-21: Sun will pass 90 degrees to natal Sun.

August 29: Moon transits past co-ruler Neptune. This date is a Saturday. Watch for any market reaction on the Friday.

August 30: Moon transits past 24 Pisces. This date is a Sunday. Watch for a possible market reaction on the Monday.

September 7: Moon transits past 14 Cancer

September 10: Moon transits past co-ruler Mars

September 2015

Key Dates

The New Moon in September occurs on the 13th with Sun at 20 degrees Virgo. The horoscope in Figure 22 depicts planetary placements several hours prior to the New Moon as the Ascendant passes 14 Cancer.

The lunation can be seen to be 150 degrees to heavy-weight planet Uranus. No other hard aspects are visible.

The lunar cycle commencing at this New Moon will run until October 12, 2015.

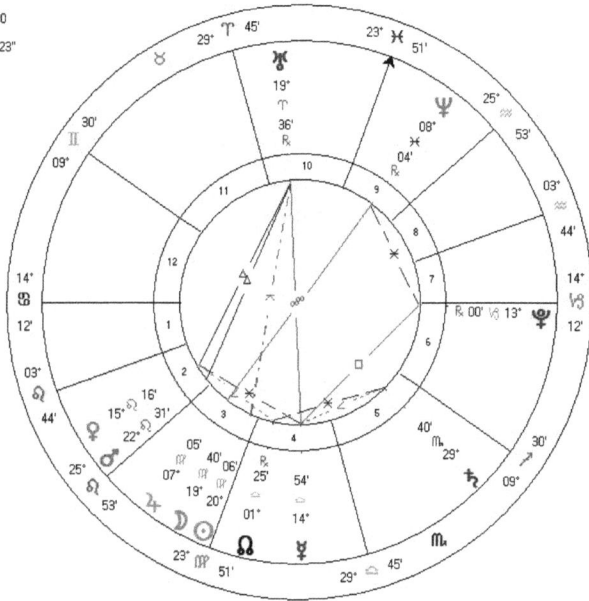

Event of 13 Sep 2015
Event Chart
13 Sep 2015, Sun
1:05:57 am EDT +4:00
New York, NY
40°N42'51" 074°W00'23"
Geocentric
Tropical
Placidus
Mean Node
Parallax Moon

Figure 22 – New Moon September 13, 2015

Key dates to be alert to during this lunation include:

Note: On September 16-17 the Federal Reserve will conduct one of its Open Market Committee meetings which will conclude with Governor Yellen speaking to the media about monetary policy.

September 26: Moon transits past co-ruler Neptune. This date is a Saturday. Watch for any market reaction on the Friday.

September 27: Moon transits past the natal MC location of 24 Pisces. This date is a Sunday. Watch for a possible market reaction on the Monday.

October 5-9: Sun transits 90 degrees to natal Asc

October 9: Moon transits past the natal Asc point at 14 Cancer

October 2015

Key Dates

The New Moon in October occurs on the 12th with Sun at 19 degrees Libra. The horoscope in Figure 23 depicts planetary placements several hours prior to the New Moon as the Ascendant passes 14 Cancer.

The lunation can be seen to be 180 degrees opposite to heavy-weight planet Uranus. This is highly suggestive of a trend change on the NYSE.

The lunar cycle commencing at this New Moon will run until November 11, 2015.

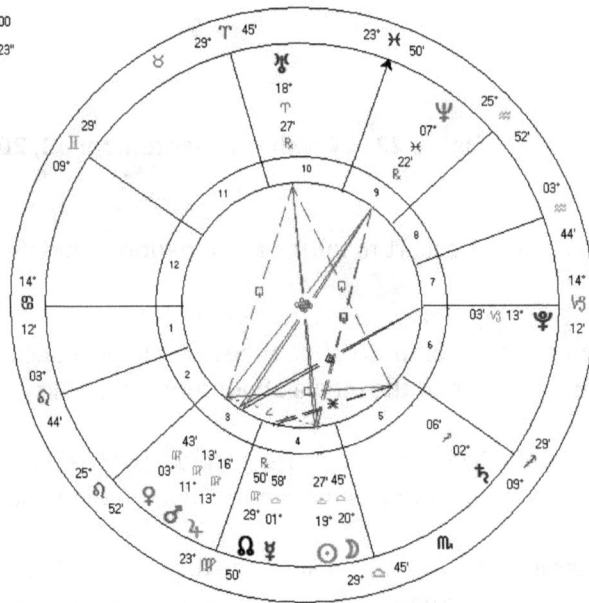

Figure 23 – New Moon October 12, 2015

Key dates to be alert to during this lunation include:

October 13-16: Sun transits 0 degrees to natal Jupiter

October 23: Moon transits past co-ruler Neptune.

October 24: Moon transits past 24 Pisces. This date is a Saturday. Watch for a possible market reaction on the Friday.

November 1: Moon transits past 14 Cancer. This date is a Sunday. Watch for a possible market reaction on the Monday.

November 6: Moon transits past co-ruler Mars

November 2015

Key Dates

The New Moon in November occurs on the 11th with Sun at 18 degrees Scorpio. The horoscope in Figure 24 depicts planetary placements several hours prior to the New Moon as the Ascendant passes 14 Cancer.

The lunation is 150 degrees to Uranus and 60 degrees favorable to Jupiter. Uranus, Jupiter and the lunation point collectively form a Yod formation which is generally regarded as a pressure point. This could have implications for a trend change or a marked increase in volatility on the NYSE.

The lunar cycle commencing at this New Moon will run until December 11, 2015.

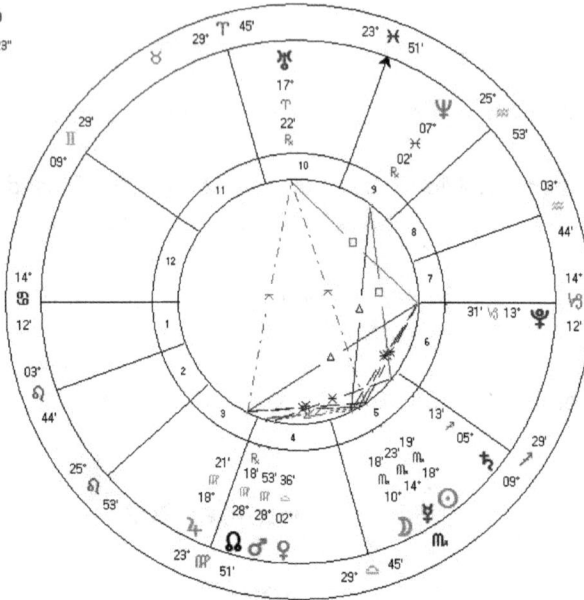

Event of 10 Nov 2015
Event Chart
10 Nov 2015, Tue
9:13:57 pm EDT +4:00
New York, NY
40°N42'51" 074°W00'23"
Geocentric
Tropical
Placidus
Mean Node
Parallax Moon

Figure 24 – New Moon November 10, 2015

Key dates to be alert to during this lunation include:

November 19: Moon transits past co-ruler Neptune.

November 20: Moon transits past 24 Pisces.

November 22-December 6: Sun will transit through a 0 degree hard aspect to Jupiter. Such hard aspects have a strong tendency to align to changes f trend on the Dow Jones Industrial Average and S&P500.

November 28: Moon transits past 14 Cancer. This date is a Saturday. Watch for a possible market reaction on the Friday.

December 5: Moon transits past co-ruler Mars. This date is a Saturday. Watch for a possible market reaction on the Friday.

December 2015

Key Dates

The New Moon in December occurs on the 11th with Sun at 18 degrees Scorpio. The horoscope in Figure 25 depicts planetary placements several hours prior to the New Moon as the Ascendant passes 14 Cancer.

The lunation is a favorable 120 degrees to Neptune and a favorable 60 degrees to Mars.

The lunar cycle commencing at this New Moon will run until January 9, 2016.

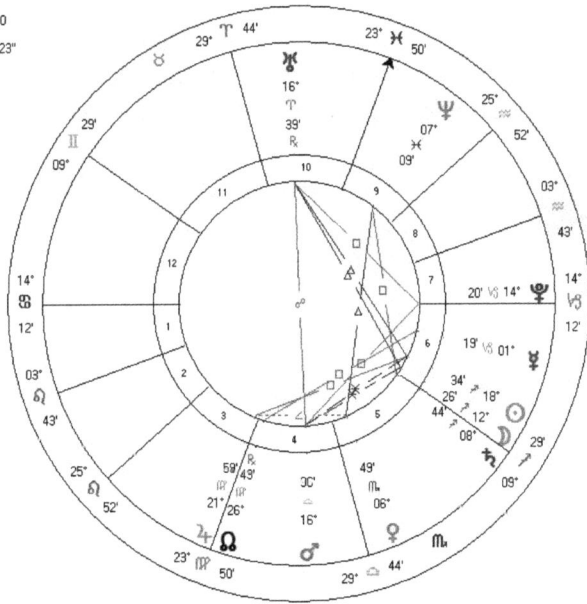

Figure 25 – New Moon December 10, 2015

Key dates to be alert to during this lunation include:

December 9-19: Sun will transit through a 90 degree hard aspect to Jupiter. Such hard aspects have a strong tendency to align to changes of trend on the Dow Jones Industrial Average and S&P500.

December 13-30: Mars transits 0 degrees to natal Jupiter

Note: On December 15-16 the Federal Reserve will conduct one of its Open Market Committee meetings which will conclude with Governor Yellen speaking to the media about monetary policy.

December 14-18: Sun passes 90 degrees to the natal MC position of the NYSE.

December 17: Moon transits past co-ruler Neptune.

December 18: Moon transits past 24 Pisces.

December 26: Moon transits past 14 Cancer. Markets will be closed for the Christmas holiday.

January 3, 2016: Moon transits past co-ruler Mars. This date is a Sunday. Watch for a possible market reaction on the Monday.

4. Astrology of Various Commodities in 2015

Gold

Gold futures started trading on the New York Mercantile Exchange on December 31, 1974.

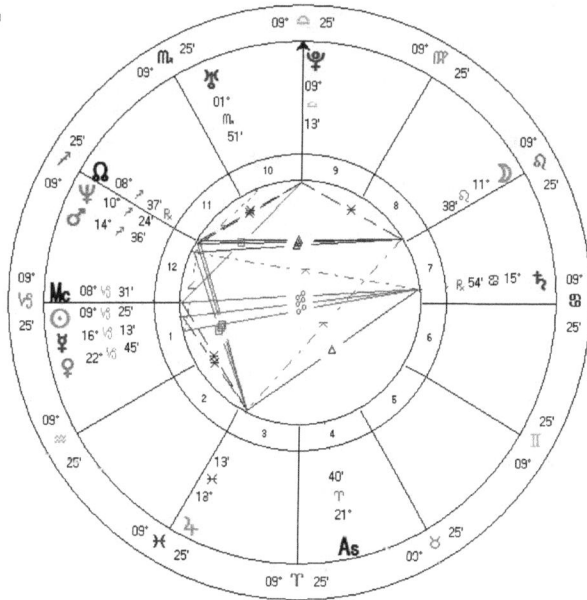

Gold Futures
Natal Chart
31 Dec 1974, Tue
11:59 am GMT +0:00
greenwich
51°N29' 000°W00'
Geocentric
Tropical
Sun on 1st
Mean Node
Parallax Moon

Figure 26 Gold futures First Trade chart

Figure 26 shows the First Trade chart for Gold futures in geocentric format. The Sun in this First Trade chart is at 9 degrees Capricorn. Jupiter is at 13 Pisces. As well, Pluto and Sun form a 90 degree hard aspect to one another. During 2015, Pluto and Sun will make hard aspects to each other on January 1, April 3, July 4 and October 4.

My research has also shown that Mars plays a significant role in the price movement of Gold futures.

The following weekly nearest futures chart in Figure 27 illustrates the impact of Mars making hard aspects to the natal Sun location at 9 Capricorn and also the impact of Mars transiting past the natal Mars location at 10 Sagittarius.

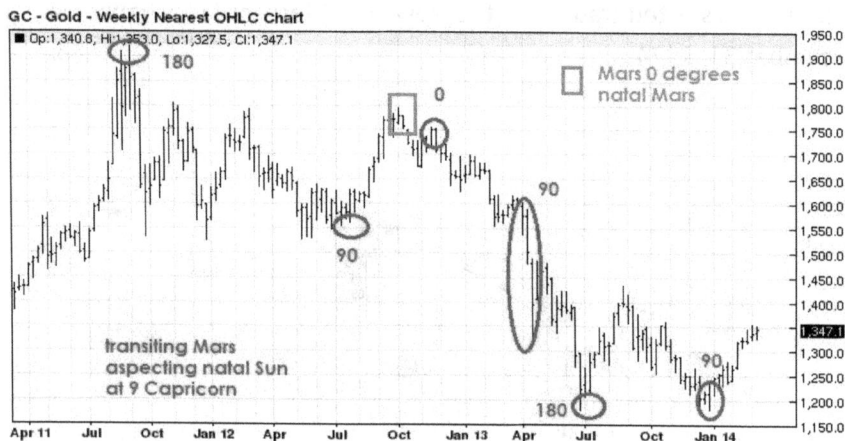

Figure 27 The Mars Influence on Gold price

For 2015, Mars will make a 90 degree hard aspect to natal Mars from January 25 through February 4.

Mars will make a 90 degree hard aspect to natal Sun from February 26 through March 9.

Mars will make a 180 degree hard aspect to natal Mars from May 27 through June 7.

Mars will make a 180 degree hard aspect to natal Sun from July 2 through July 14.

Mars will make a 90 degree hard aspect to natal Mars from October 11 through October 24.

Mars will make a 90 degree hard aspect to natal Sun from November 21 through December 5.

My research further suggests that Mercury Retrograde events and maximum Elongation events should be watched closely as Gold does have a tendency to exhibit price inflection points in conjunction with these Mercury phenomena.

The daily nearest chart in Figure 28 illustrates the connection between these Mercury phenomena and Gold prices.

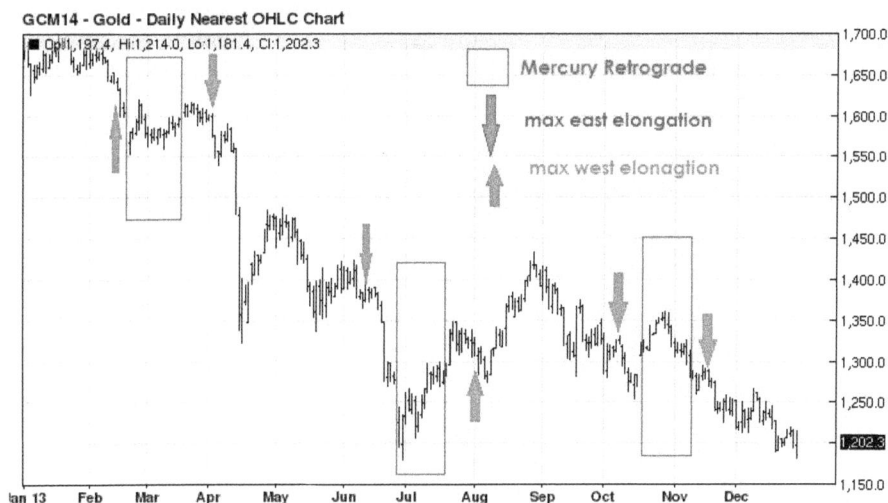

Figure 28 Gold and the Mercury Influence

For 2015, Mercury will be Retrograde from January 22 through February 10, from May 19 through June 11 and from September 18 through October 9.

For 2015, Mercury will experience elongation maxima on January 14 and February 24, again on May 7 and June 24, again on September 4 and October 16 and finally on December 29.

Silver

Silver futures started trading on a recognized financial exchange in 1933. Figure 29 shows the First Trade chart for Silver futures in geocentric format.

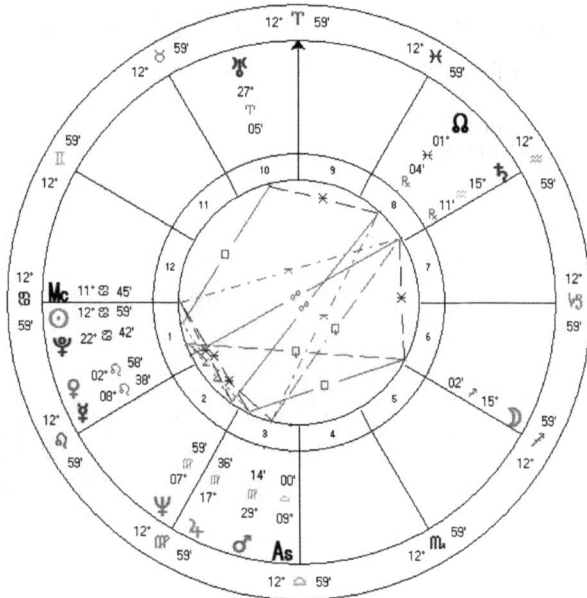

Figure 29 Silver futures First Trade chart

The Sun in this chart is at 12 Cancer and Jupiter is at 17 Virgo. The Sun is at a favorable 60 degrees to Jupiter. Note that the Moon is within a day and a bit of being 180 degrees opposite Sun (ie a Full Moon).

My research has shown that times when transiting Sun, transiting Mars and transiting Jupiter make hard aspects to natal Sun should be watched carefully for evidence of trend changes and price inflection points.

Figure 30 Silver and Astro Events

The weekly nearest chart in Figure 30 illustrates the importance of these hard aspects. The daily nearest chart in Figure 31 provides a more detailed examination.

Figure 31 A More Detailed Astro Examination of Silver

Planetary declinations should also be considered when studying price action of Silver futures. In particular the declination maxima and minima

67

of Mars and also of Sun should be watched. Figure 32 illustrates the effect of these declination events.

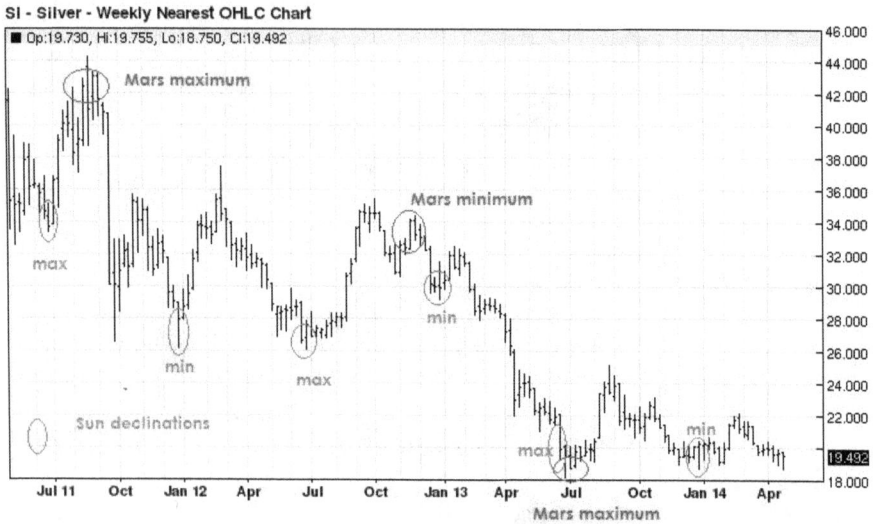

SI - Silver - Weekly Nearest OHLC Chart

Figure 32 Planetary declinations and Silver prices

Lastly, Silver and Moon phases should also be watched carefully. Silver prices at New and Full Moons should be watched for possible trend changes or price inflection points. The daily nearest futures chart in Figure 33 illustrates this concept.

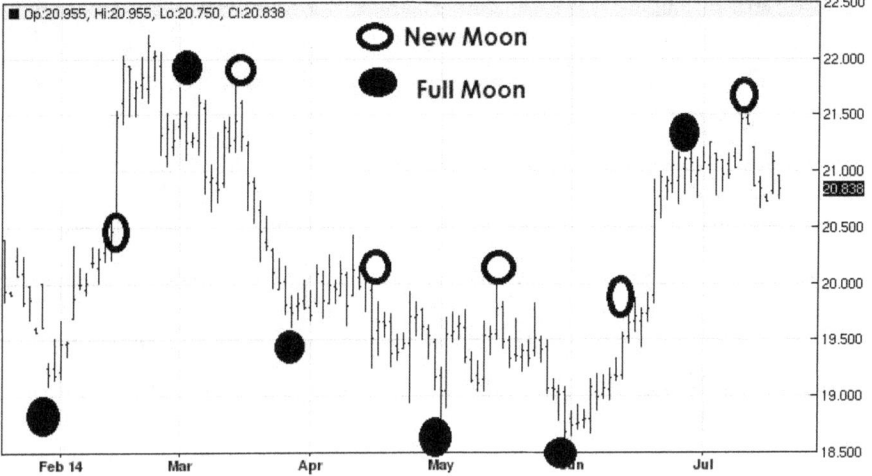

Figure 33 Silver prices at New and Full Moons

For 2015, Sun will make a 180 degree aspect to natal Sun from January 1 through January 7.

Mars will make a 90 degree aspect to natal Sun from March 2 through March 13.

Sun will make a 90 degree aspect to natal Sun from March 29 through April 6.

Sun will make a 0 degree aspect to natal Sun from June 30 through July 9.

Mars will make a 0 degree aspect to Sun from July 6 through July 19. This overlap of Sun and Mars both making aspects suggests that this period will see some critical price developments on Silver and Silver related mining equities.

Sun will make a 90 degree aspect to Natal Sun from September 30 through October 9.

Mars will make a 90 degree aspect to natal sun from November 25 through December 10.

For 2015, Mars will record its absolute maximum declination for the year from June 2 through July 21. This timeframe should be watched carefully as it overlaps with the astro event of Sun and Mars both being 0 degrees conjunct to natal Sun.

For 2015, as with all years, Sun will record its maximum declination on either side of the June 21 Summer Solstice. Sun will record its minimum declination on either side of the December 21 Winter Solstice.

For 2015, New Moon dates are January 5, February 3, March 5, April 4, May 4, June 2, July 2, July 31, August 29, September 28, October 27, November 25 and December 25.

For 2015, Full Moon dates are January 20, February 18, March 20, April 18, May 18, June 16, July 16, August 14, September 13, October 13, November 11 and December 11.

Copper

The First Trade Date for Copper futures was July 29, 1988. Figure 25 illustrates the First Trade chart in geocentric format.

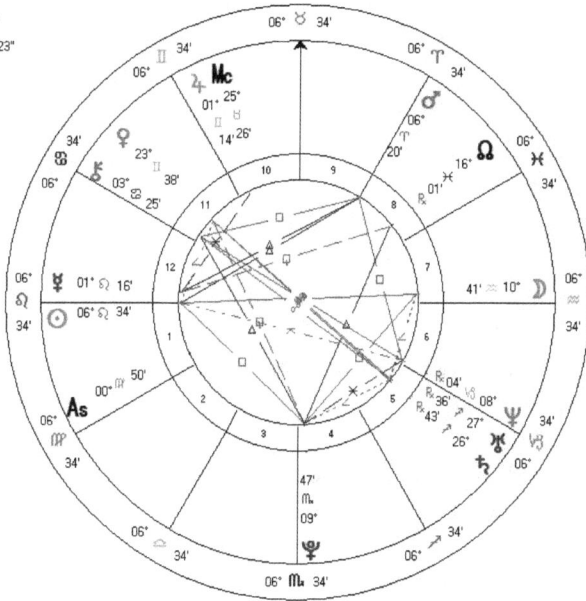

Figure 34 Copper futures First Trade chart

The 1974 First Trade chart for Gold futures displayed a Sun-Pluto 90 degree aspect. In the Copper First Trade chart from July 29, 1988, notice how Pluto and Sun are also at a 90 degree aspect to each other. It is certainly curious how two futures contracts making their debuts onto recognized exchanges fourteen years apart could have the same aspect in play. In my opinion, the individuals in charge of the regulatory bodies that determine First Trade dates are more versed in Astrology than we may think.

Also, notice in this chart that the first Trade date is that of a New Moon.

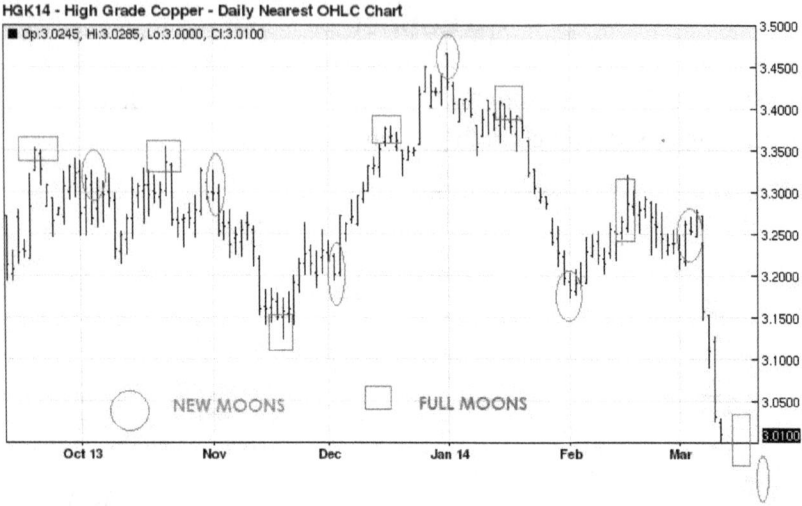

HGK14 - High Grade Copper - Daily Nearest OHLC Chart

Figure 35 Copper price inflection points and Moon phase

The daily nearest price chart for Copper futures in Figure 35 illustrates the importance of Full and New Moons. Notice how price tends to pivot at the time immediately before and after New and Full Moons. If you are trading Copper futures or if you are short-term trading Copper-mining related equities you should be able to use the Moon to your advantage.

Hard aspects between transiting Sun and natal Pluto can also offer unique insight into Copper price fluctuations. The weekly nearest Copper futures chart in Figure 36 illustrates further.

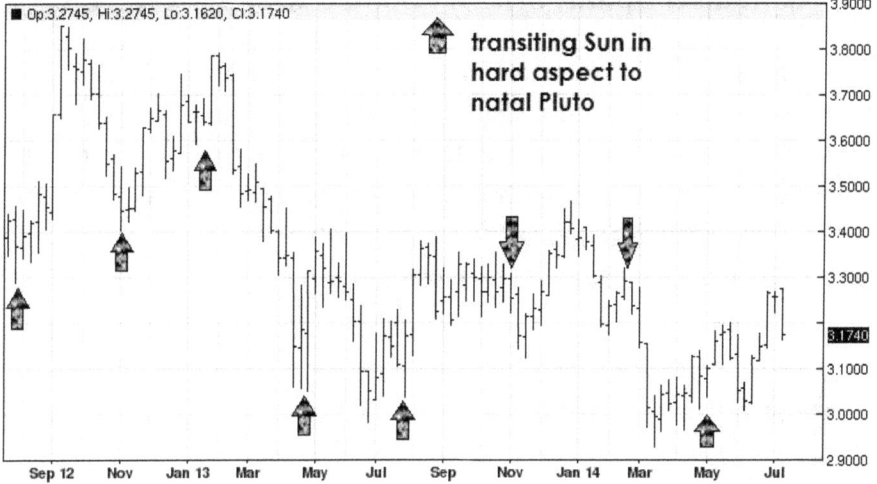

HG - High Grade Copper - Weekly Nearest OHLC Chart

Op:3.2745, Hi:3.2745, Lo:3.1620, Cl:3.1740

transiting Sun in
hard aspect to
natal Pluto

Figure 36 Copper inflection points and Sun-Pluto hard aspects

For 2015, New Moon dates are January 5, February 3, March 5, April 4, May 4, June 2, July 2, July 31, August 29, September 28, October 27, November 25 and December 25.

For 2015, Full Moon dates are January 20, February 18, March 20, April 18, May 18, June 16, July 16, August 14, September 13, October 13, November 11 and December 11.

For 2015, transiting Sun will make a 180 degree hard aspect to natal Pluto from January 22 through January 30.

For 2015, transiting Sun will make a 90 degree hard aspect to natal Pluto from April 22 through May 1 and October 26 through November 3.

For 2015, transiting Sun will make a 0 degree hard aspect to natal Pluto from July 25 through August 2.

Canadian Dollar, British Pound and Japanese Yen

These three futures instruments all started trading on May 16th, 1972 at the Chicago Mercantile Exchange. The horoscope in Figure 37 illustrates planetary placements at this date. There are no significant aspects to the Sun evident in this horoscope. It is interesting to note, however, that Mars is 180 degrees opposite Jupiter. This suggests that Mars and Jupiter may play a role in price fluctuations on these currencies.

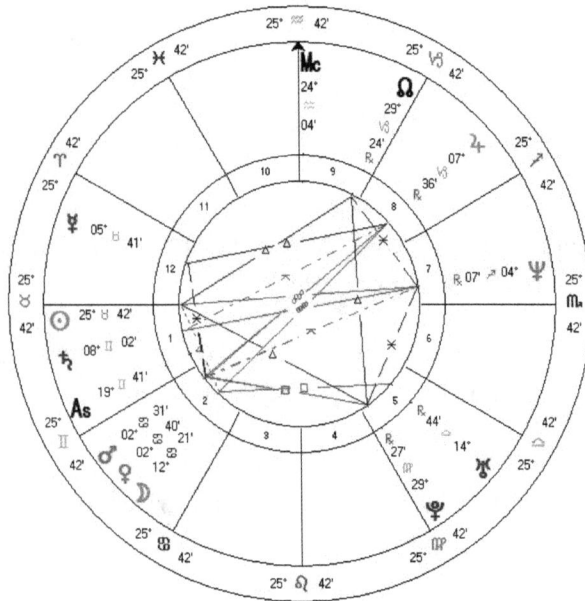

Figure 37 Pound, Yen, Canadian First Trade chart

The chart in Figure 38 illustrates daily nearest futures price action on the British Pound. The chart has been overlaid with various Mars, Jupiter and Sun astro events. Note the correlation to price inflection points. The one caveat is that these astro events do take several days to unfold. Each of these currencies can be seen to respond to these astro events, just not all on the same exact day.

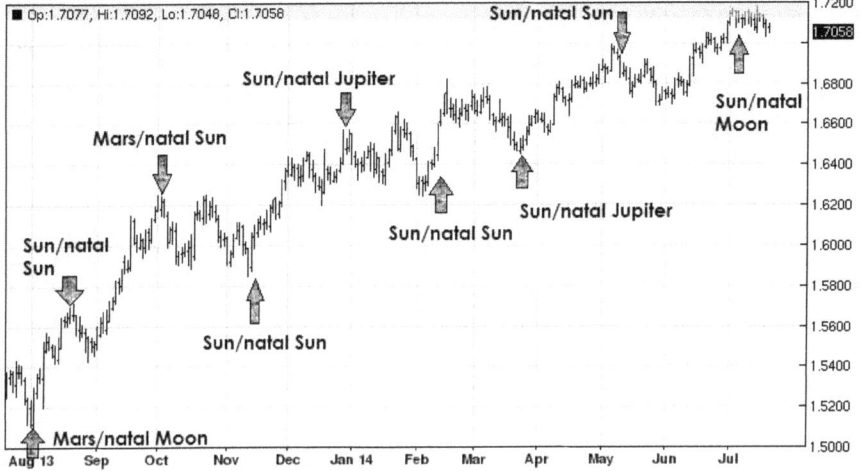

Figure 38 Daily nearest British Pound price with astro events

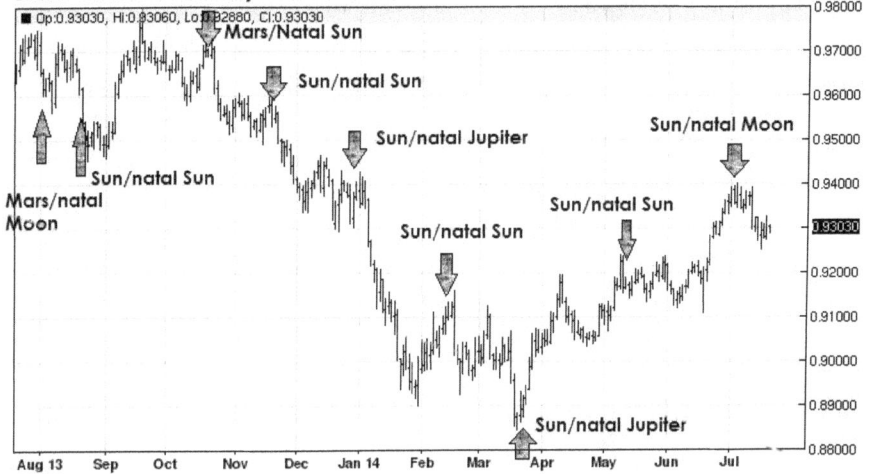

Figure 39 Daily nearest Canadian Dollar price with astro events

The chart in Figure 39 illustrates daily nearest futures price action for the Canadian dollar. These same astro events have been overlaid on a chart of the Yen as shown in Figure 40.

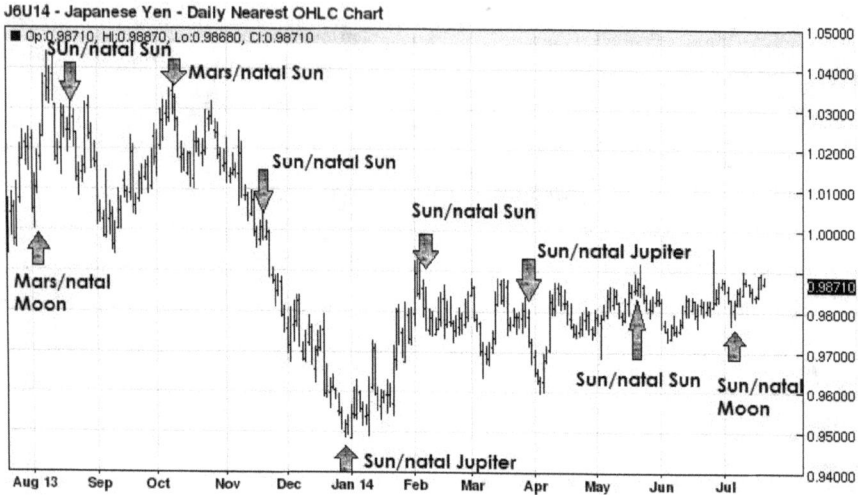

Figure 40 Daily nearest Yen futures price with astro events

For 2015, the period leading up to and including January 2 will see Sun complete a 0 degree conjunction to natal Jupiter. This is followed by a Mars 90 degree natal Sun aspect from January 2 through January 10.

February 10 through February 18 will see Sun make a 90 degree aspect to natal Sun.

February 25 through March 5 will see Mars make a 90 degree aspect to natal Jupiter. March 3 through March 12 will see Mars make a 90 degree aspect to natal Moon.

March 25 through April 1 will see Sun make a 90 degree aspect to natal Jupiter.

May 1 through May 11 will see Mars make a 0 degree aspect to natal Sun.

May 12 through May 20 will see Sun make a 0 degree conjunction to natal Sun. The month of May should be a very active time for these currencies.

July 7 through July 19 will have Mars making a 0 degree aspect to natal Moon.

July 6 through August 6 will have Jupiter making a 90 degree aspect to natal Sun.

August 14 to August 22 will see Sun making a 90 degree aspect to natal Sun.

September 11 through September 24 will see Mars making a 90 degree aspect to natal Sun.

November 14 through November 22 will have Sun passing 180 degrees to natal Sun.

Finally, December 25 through January 2, 2016 will have Sun passing 0 degrees to natal Jupiter.

Those periods in 2015 when Mercury and Venus are Retrograde should also be watched for possible trend changes too. The chart of the British Pound futures in Figure 41 illustrates past Retrograde events.

B6U14 - British Pound - Daily Nearest OHLC Chart

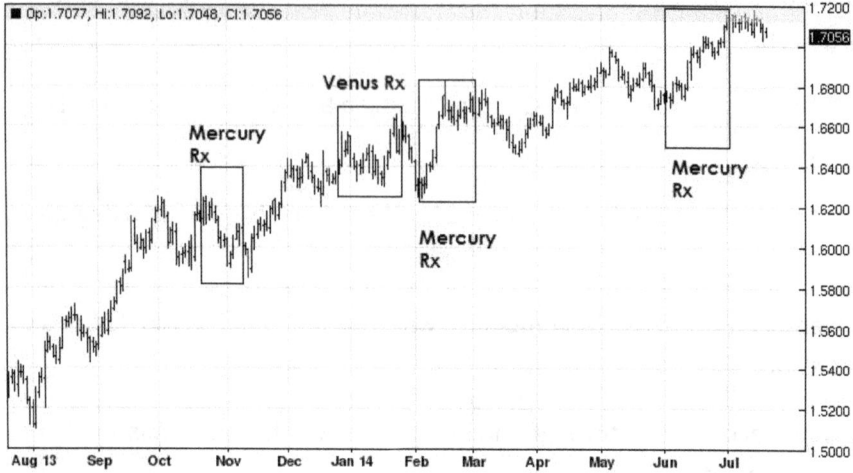

Figure 41 Effect of Retrograde events on Currencies

As this chart shows, Mercury Retrograde events can contain sharp rises and falls in currency price. Note also that the Venus retrograde event in early 2014 was followed by a sharp drop in currency value.

For 2015, Mercury will be Retrograde from:

January 22 through February 10
May 19 through June 11
September 18 through October 9

Euro Currency Futures

The Euro became the official currency for the European Union on January 1, 2002. A look at the geocentric natal First Trade chart for this date in Figure 42 reveals a Sun conjunction to Venus and a 180 degree opposition to Jupiter.

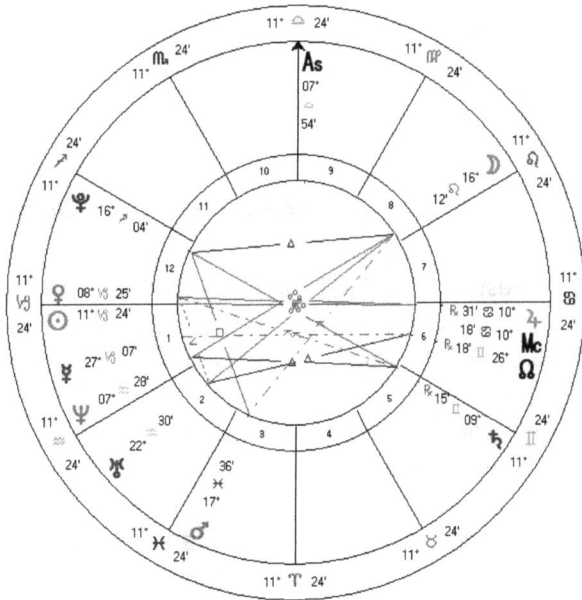

Figure 42 Euro Currency First Trade chart

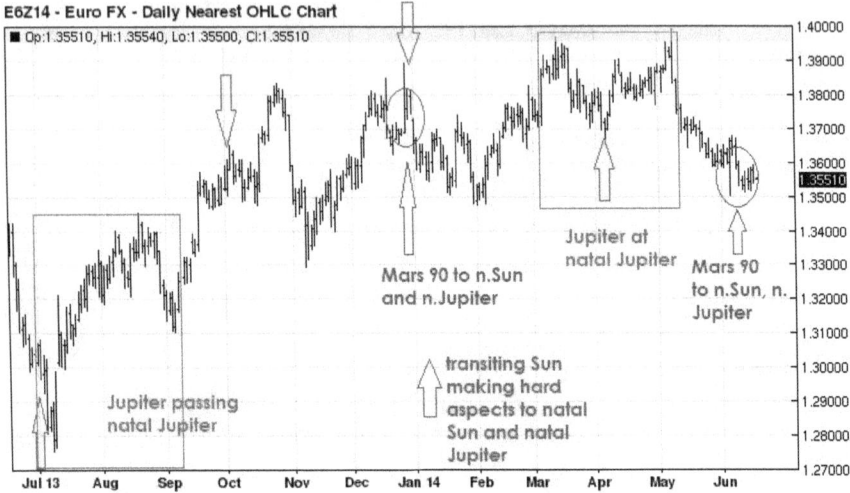

Figure 43 Astro events and the Euro Currency

The daily nearest chart in Figure 43 illustrates the recent effects of Jupiter on the Euro. This chart also shows how transiting Sun and transiting Mars making hard aspects to natal Sun and natal Jupiter affect the Euro.

For 2015, the period late December 2014 through January 6, 2015 will see Sun make a 0 degree aspect to natal Sun.

February 28 through March 10 will see Mars make a 90 degree aspect to natal Jupiter. This period overlaps the timespan March 2 through March 10 when Mars will pass 90 degrees to natal Sun.

March 27 through April 5 will see Sun at 90 degrees natal Sun.

April 17 through April 28 will see Mars pass 90 degrees natal Moon.

May 3 through May 11 will see Sun pass 90 degrees to natal moon.

May 7 through June 22 could be volatile as Jupiter passes 0 degrees to natal Moon.

June 30 through July 7 will have Sun at 180 degrees to natal Sun. Sun will also be at a 0 degree aspect to natal Jupiter at this time too.

July 7 through July 17 will see Mars at 180 degrees natal Sun and 0 degrees natal Jupiter.

August 5 through August 13 will have Sun at 0 degrees natal Moon.

August 28 through September 9 will have Mars 0 degrees natal Moon.

October 2 through October 10 will have Sun 90 degrees natal Sun.

November 5 through November 13 will have Sun 90 degrees natal Moon.

November 26 through December 10 will have Mars 90 degrees natal Sun.

Finally, late December will make the start of Sun passing 0 degrees natal Sun.

Australian Dollar

Australian dollar futures started trading on the Chicago Mercantile Exchange on January 13, 1987. As the horoscope in Figure 44 shows, Sun and Mercury are conjunct at 22-23 degrees Capricorn.

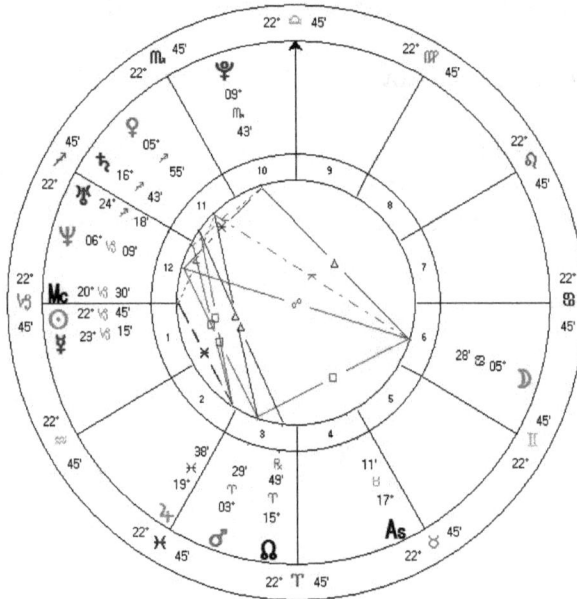

Figure 44 First Trade Chart for Australian Dollar Futures

The Australian Dollar bears a close affinity to actions of Mercury. The chart in Figure 45 illustrates daily nearest price action on Australian dollar futures. This chart has been overlaid with those instances where transiting Mercury made 0, 30, 60, 90, 120 and 180 degree aspects to natal Sun. This chart has also been marked with those times when Mercury exhibited Retrograde motion.

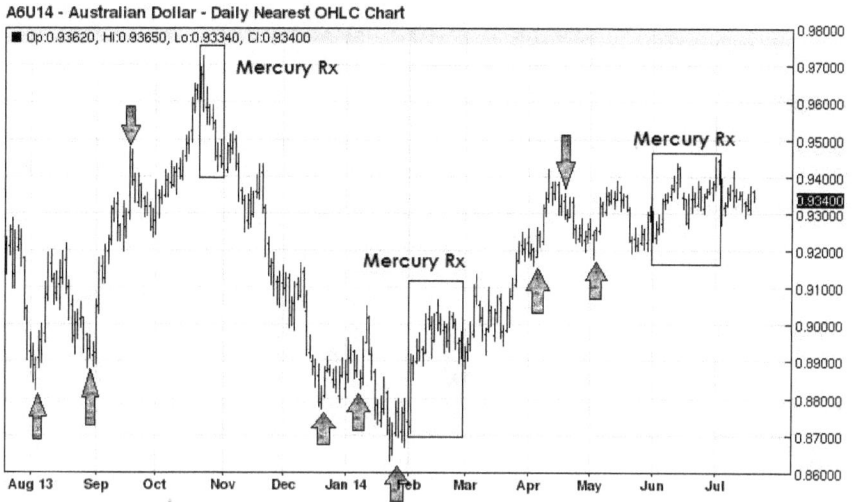

Figure 45 Australian Dollar futures and Mercury

For 2015, Mercury will be Retrograde from:

January 22 through February 10
May 19 through June 11
September 18 through October 9

For 2015, Mercury will make 0, 90, 120 and 180 degree aspects to natal Sun on:

December 29, 2014 through January 2, 2015
March 6 through March 10
April 10 through April 12
April 24 through 28
July 18 through July 21
August 20 through August 24
October 26 through October 30
November 14 through November 18
December 3 through December 7
December 23 through December 29

30 Year Bond Futures

30 Year Bond futures started trading in Chicago on August 22, 1977. Figure 46 presents the geocentric natal chart for this date.

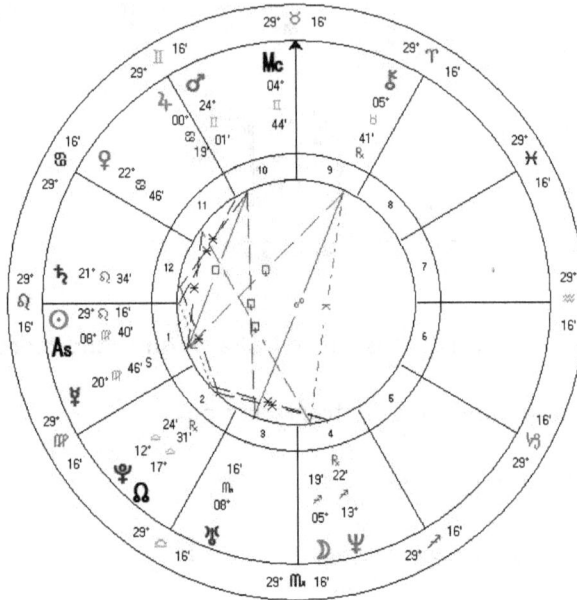

Figure 46 First Trade chart for 30 Year Bond futures

The astro events that affect Bond prices are similar to many of those examined to this point. The chart in Figure 47 illustrates daily nearest price action on Bond futures. Several astro events have been overlaid on the chart.

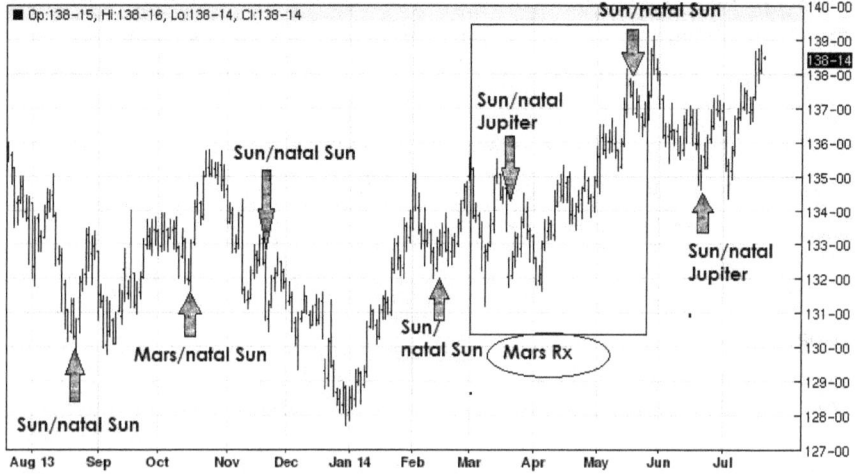

Figure 47 Bond futures and Astro events

My research has also shown that New Moons and Full Moons affect Bond prices.

The chart in Figure 48 presents daily nearest price data with New Moon and Full Moon dates indicated.

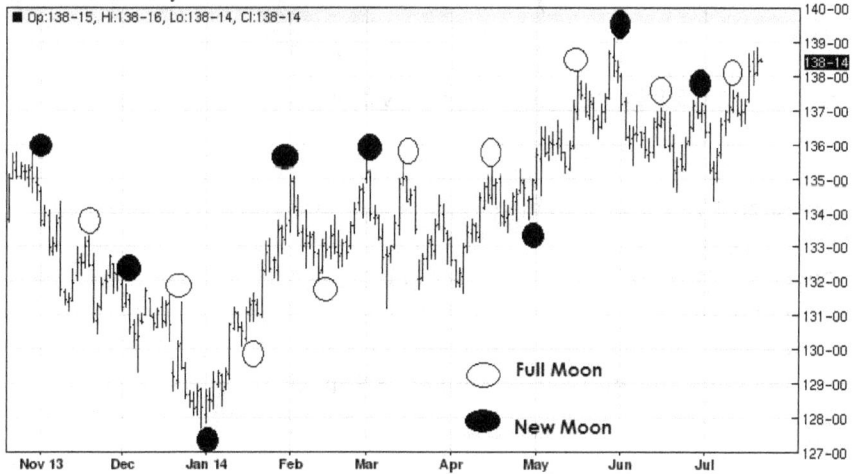

Figure 48 Bond Futures and Lunar events

For 2015, New Moon dates are January 5, February 3, March 5, April 4, May 4, June 2, July 2, July 31, August 29, September 28, October 27, November 25 and December 25.

For 2015, Full Moon dates are January 20, February 18, March 20, April 18, May 18, June 16, July 16, August 14, September 13, October 13, November 11 and December 11.

For 2015, Mars will be 180 degrees to natal Sun from January 7 through January 15.

From February 15 through February 21 Sun will be 180 degrees natal Sun

From February 18 through February 24 Mars will be 90 degrees natal Jupiter.

From March 19 through March 22 Sun will be 90 degrees natal Jupiter

From May 7 through May 15 Mars will be 90 degrees natal Sun

From May 17 through May 23 Sun will be 90 degrees natal Sun

From June 19 through June 29 Sun and Mars both will transit past a 0 degree aspect to natal Sun. This could be a significant time for Bond prices.

From July 18 through August 30 Jupiter will slowly move past 0 degrees natal Sun.

From August 18 through August 27, Sun will transit 0 degrees natal Sun

From September 19 through October 1, Mars will make a 0 degree aspect to natal Jupiter.

From November 17 through November 25 Sun will make a 90 degree aspect to natal Sun.

The Bond story has one additional layer to it. Authors Jeanne Long and Larry Pesavento, whose material I have researched for my previous books, are adamant that changes in Bond prices can be seen to align to geocentric Mars changing signs of the zodiac. Mars will change signs approximately every seven weeks. The reason for this correlation to sign changes remains unclear to me. My research has shown that this phenomenon does align to trend changes, but not with 100% correlation.

For 2015, geocentric Mars will change signs of the zodiac on January 13 when it moves into Pisces.

February 21 will see a move into Aries.

April 1 will see a move into Taurus.

May 13 will see a move into Gemini.

June 25 will see a move into Cancer.

August 9 will see a move into Leo.

September 26 will see a move into Virgo.

November 13 will see a move into Libra.

January 4, 2016 will see a move into Scorpio.

Wheat, Corn, Oats

Wheat, Corn and Oats futures all share the same first trade date from 1877. The horoscope in Figure 49 shows planetary placements at this date.

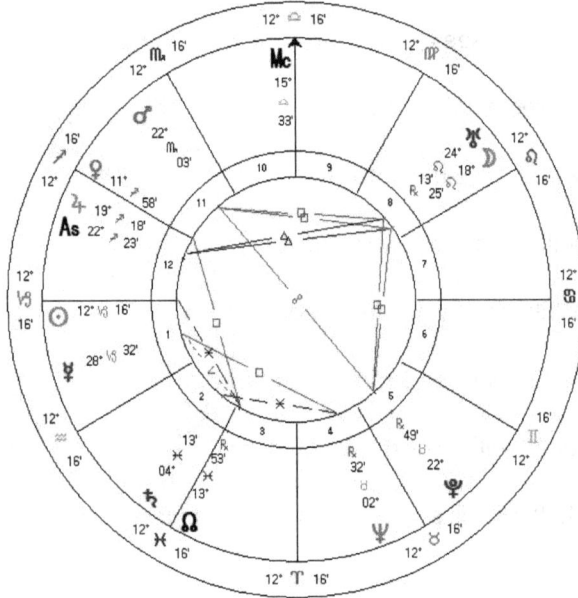

Wheat, Corn, Oats Natal (GEO)
Natal Chart
2 Jan 1877 NS, Tue
11:59 am GMT +0:00
Chicago, Illinois
41°N51' 087°W39'
Geocentric
Tropical
Sun on 1st
Mean Node
Parallax Moon

Figure 49 First Trade chart for Wheat, Corn and Oats futures

The chart in Figure 50 illustrates daily nearest price action for Corn futures. This chart has been overlaid with various astro events that align to price pivot points. What I have not overlaid on this chart is an astro phenomenon that will not be seen again for many years to come. Heavyweight planet Uranus is making a 90 degree hard aspect to natal Sun. This seems to account for the negative emotions towards Corn. This aspect will not be fully out of the way until Q1 2015. The chart in Figure 51 illustrates daily nearest price action for Wheat futures. This chart has been overlaid with various astro events that align to price pivot points. The same comments concerning Uranus 90 degrees natal Sun apply to Wheat.

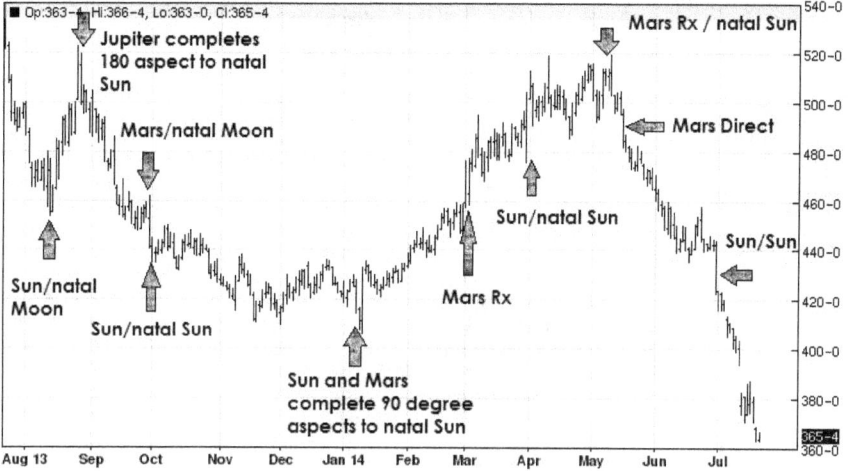

ZCZ14 - Corn - Daily Nearest OHLC Chart

Figure 50 Corn prices and astro events

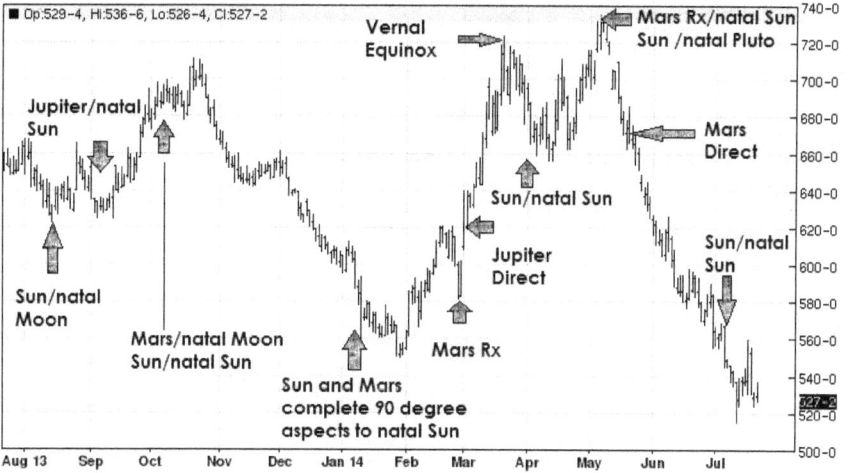

ZWZ14 - Wheat - Daily Nearest OHLC Chart

Figure 51 Wheat prices and astro events

My research has also shown that Mercury plays a role in price pivot points on the grains. The daily nearest chart of Wheat futures in Figure 52 has been overlaid with Mercury 0,30,60,90 and 120 degree aspects to natal Sun as well as Mercury retrograde events. As the chart in Figure 53 shows, Corn exhibits a similar sensitivity to Mercury events.

89

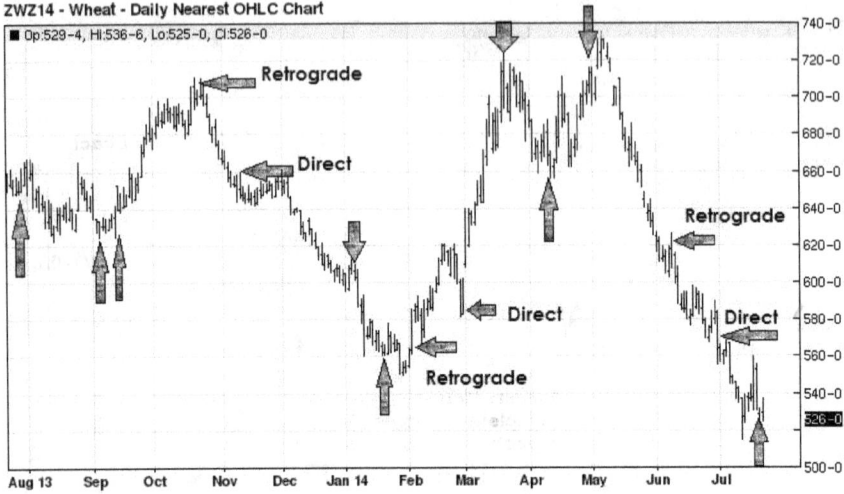

Figure 52 Wheat prices and Mercury events

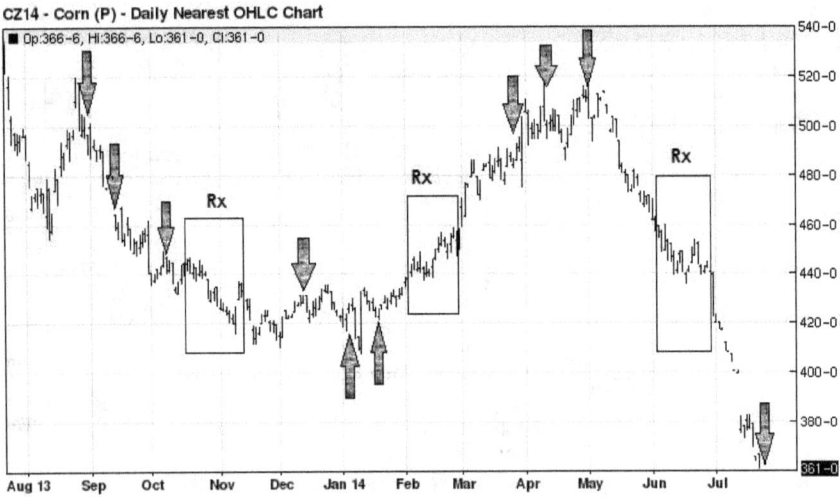

Figure 53 Corn prices and Mercury events

For 2015, transiting Sun will be 0 degree to natal Sun from January 1 through January 6.

Mars will be 90 degrees natal Sun from March 4 through March 12.

Sun will be 90 degrees natal Sun from March 30 through April 5.

Sun will be 180 degrees natal Sun from July 1 through July 7.

Mars will follow closely behind with a 180 degree aspect to natal Sun from July 8 through July 17.

From June 20 through July 20, Jupiter will pass 0 degrees to natal Moon. Watch for added volatility in this timeframe.

Sun will be 90 degrees natal Sun from October 2 through October 9.

Mars will be 90 degrees natal Sun from November 28 through December 8.

For 2015, Mercury will be Retrograde from:

January 22 through February 10
May 19 through June 11
September 18 through October 9

For 2015, Mercury will make 0, 90, 120 and 180 degree aspects to natal Sun on:

January 12, 2014 through January 16, 2015
February 26 through March 1
March 19 through March 21
April 5 through April 7
April 20 through April 22
July 13 through July 16
August 13 through August 15
September 6 through September 11
November 8 through November 11
November 27 through November 30
December 17 through December 19

Soybeans

Soybean futures started trading on a recognized exchange in October 1936. The horoscope in Figure 54 illustrates the planetary placements at that time. What I find intriguing is the location of the Sun. Notice how it is exactly 90 degrees to the location of the Sun in the First Trade chart for Wheat, Corn and Oats? As I have previously noted, the regulatory officials who determine these First Trade dates seem to know more about Astrology trilogy may think.

Figure 54 Soybeans First Trade chart

The chart in Figure 55 illustrates daily nearest price action on Soybean futures. This chart has been overlaid with various astro events.

ZSX14 - Soybeans - Daily Nearest OHLC Chart

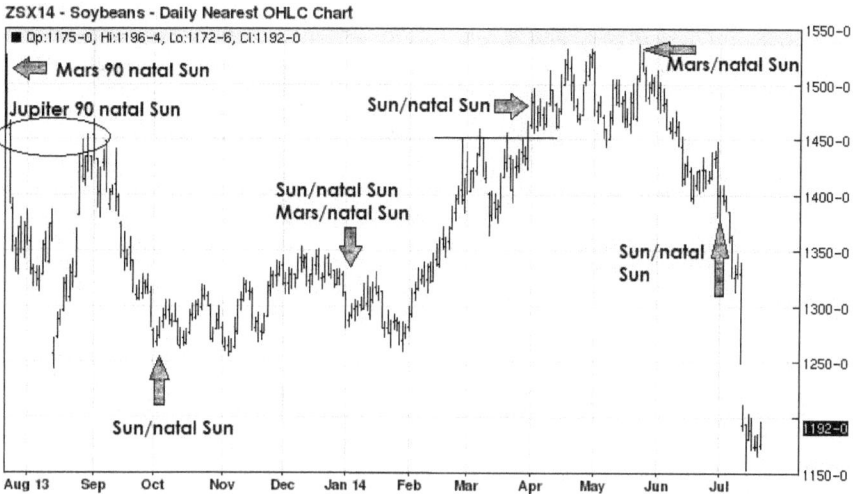

Figure 55 Soybeans and astro events

What is not overlaid on this chart is an astro phenomenon that will not be seen again for many years to come. Heavy-weight planet Uranus is currently making a 180 degree hard aspect to natal Sun. This seems to be adding to the negative emotions towards Beans. This Uranus transit will not be out of the way until Q1 of 2015. Also not shown on this chart is the 90 degree aspect between Jupiter and natal Sun. Such hard aspects occur only every 3 years or so. In this case, the price peak in early May aligns to the completion of this aspect. Jupiter's next hard aspect to natal Sun is in 2017.

For 2015, transiting Sun will make a 90 degree aspect to natal Sun from December 31, 2014 through January 5, 2015.

Transiting Sun will make a 180 degree aspect to natal Sun from March 31 through April 4.

A 90 degree aspect to natal Sun will occur from July 2 through July 7.

A 0 degree aspect will occur from October 3 through October 8.

Transiting Mars will make a 180 degree aspect to natal Sun from March 5 through March 10.

Mars will be 90 degrees natal Sun from July 9 through July 15.

Mars will be 0 degrees natal Sun from November 29 through December 6.

From December 31 through January 5, Mars will be 90 degrees natal Sun. Soybeans are affected by Mercury making 0,30,60,90,120 and 180 degree aspects to natal Sun. Mercury Retrograde events also contribute to the price behavior of Soybeans. The daily nearest chart in Figure 56 illustrates the Mercury effect.

Figure 56 Soybeans and Mercury events

For 2015, Mercury will be Retrograde from:

January 22 through February 10
May 19 through June 11
September 18 through October 9

For 2015, Mercury will make 120 degree aspects to natal Sun from January 11 through January 15 and again from February 24 through March 1.

A 180 degree aspect will occur from April 4 through April 6.

Mercury will make 120 degree aspects from May 10 through May 18 and June 24 through June 27.

Mercury will make a 90 degree aspect to natal Sun from July 13 through July 15.

A 60 degree aspect will follow from July 28 through July 30.

A 30 degree aspect will occur from August 14 through August 16.

Mercury will make a 0 degree aspect to natal Sun from September 6 through September 10 and from October 20 through October 23.

A 30 degree aspect will occur from November 8 through November 10.

A 60 degree aspect will follow from November 27 through November 28.

Finally, a 90 degree aspect will occur from December 16 through December 18.

Soybeans also have a tendency to record price trend changes in proximity to New Moons as the daily nearest futures chart in Figure XX illustrates.

Figure 57 Soybeans and New Moons

For 2015, New Moon dates are January 5, February 3, March 5, April 4, May 4, June 2, July 2, July 31, August 29, September 28, October 27, November 25 and December 25.

Crude Oil

Crude Oil futures started trading for the first time in March 1983. A unique alignment of celestial points can be seen in the horoscope in Figure 58. Notice how Mars, North Node, (Saturn/Pluto) and Neptune form a rectangle.

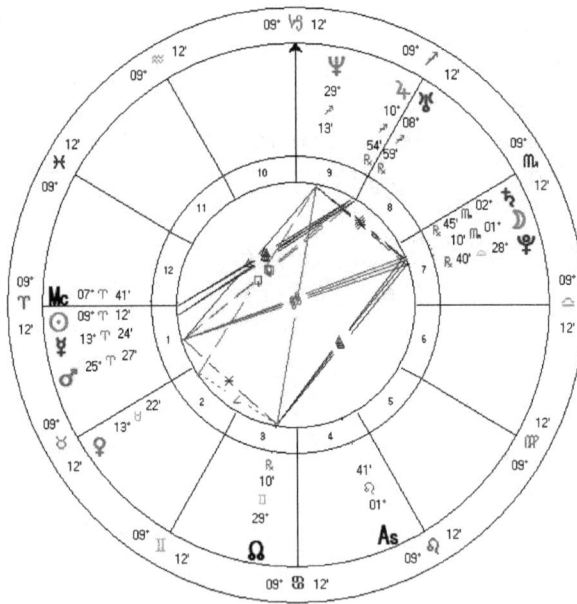

Figure 58 Crude Oil First Trade chart

The chart in Figure 59 illustrates daily nearest price action on Crude Oil futures. This chart has been overlaid with various astro events. As this chart might suggest, Crude Oil is a complex instrument to analyse with astro events. The usual Sun / natal Sun aspects come into play as do Mars/natal Sun events. Where Crude gets complex is when the rectangle corner points in the First Trade chart make aspects to transiting Sun and/or Mars.

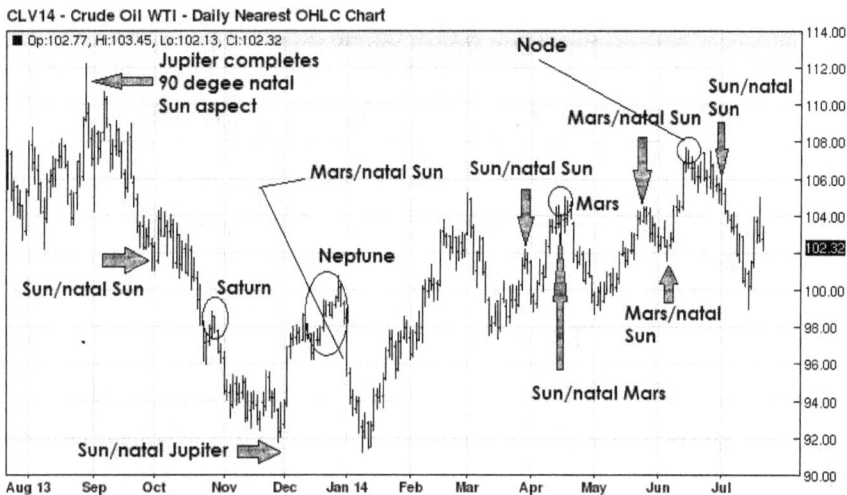

CLV14 - Crude Oil WTI - Daily Nearest OHLC Chart

Figure 59 Crude Oil astro events

For 2015, these four corners of the rectangle will be aspected as follows:

Mars will pass the Mars location at 25 Aries from March 21 through March 29.

Sun will pass the Mars location from April 12 through April 18.

Sun and Mars will pass the Node location at 29 Gemini from June 17 through June 26.

Sun will pass the Saturn location at 2 Scorpio from October 23 through October 29.

Sun will pass the Neptune location at 29 Sagittarius from December 18 through December 25.

For 2015, Sun will make a 90 degree square aspect to natal Sun from late December 2015 through January 3, 2015.

Mars will make a 0 degree aspect to natal Sun from February 28 through March 8.

Sun will be 0 degrees natal Sun from March 27 through April 2.

Sun will be 90 degrees natal Sun from June 28 through July 4.

Mars will follow right behind with a 90 degree aspect to natal Sun from July 4 through July 12.

Sun will make a 180 degree aspect to natal Sun from September 29 through October 6.

Mars will make a 180 degree aspect to natal Sun from November 23 through December 3.

From late December through to January 3, 2016 Sun will make a 90 degree aspect to natal Sun.

My studies have shown that Crude Oil is influenced by Mercury as well. The daily nearest futures chart in Figure 60 illustrates this effect.

Notice how times when transiting Mercury makes hard aspects to natal Sun, Crude Oil price action tends towards an inflection point. Mercury Retrograde events either contain a trend inflection point or are closely related in time to an inflection point. Note further that inflection points in price result as Mercury passes by 0 degrees to the four corner points of the rectangle in the First Trade chart.

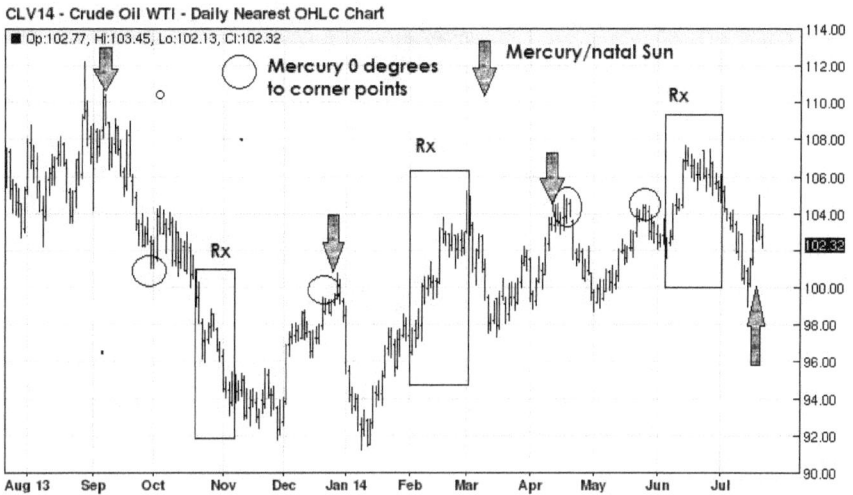

Figure 60 Crude Oil and Mercury events

For 2015, Mercury will be Retrograde from:

January 22 through February 10
May 19 through June 11
September 18 through October 9

For 2015, Mercury will make a 0 degree aspect to natal Sun from April 3 through April 6.

Mercury will make a 90 degree aspect to natal Sun from July 11 through July 14.

A 180 degree aspect will unfold from September 1 through September 7.

As Mercury turns Direct again, it will pass by 180 degrees to natal Sun again from October 17 through October 21.

Mercury will finish up the calendar year with a 90 degree aspect to natal Sun from December 13 through December 17.

Mercury will pass by the four corners of the natal chart rectangle on April 11-13, July 7-10 and November 20-24.

Coffee

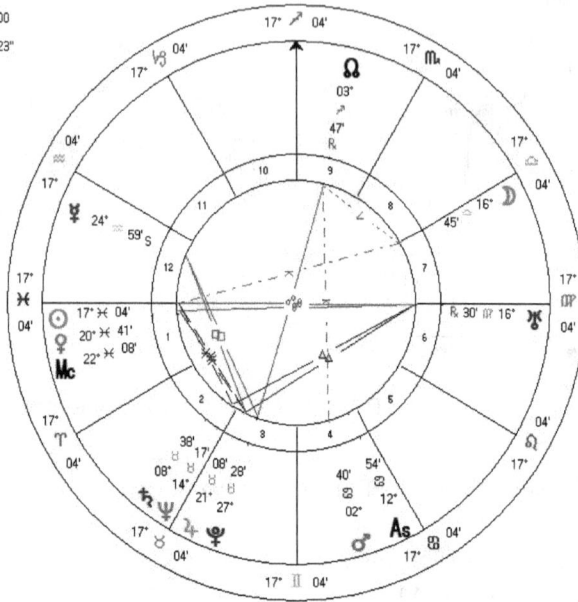

Coffee
Natal Chart
7 Mar 1882 NS, Tue
12:25:54 pm EST +5:00
New York, NY
40°N42'51" 074°W00'23"
Geocentric
Tropical
Sun on 1st
Mean Node
Parallax Moon

Figure 61 Coffee futures First Trade chart

Coffee futures started trading in New York in early March of 1882. The horoscope wheel in Figure 61 illustrates planetary placements at that time.

In the Coffee horoscope, note the 180 degree aspect between Sun and Uranus. The McWhirter methodology cautions that it is not wise to invest in situations where this sort of aspect exists because one will experience many wild ups and downs in price over time. A quick look at a 10 year price chart of Coffee reveals a price range of $0.65/pound to $3.06/pound with many wild swings.

Venus astro events have an effect on price action of Coffee futures. This is likely the case due to the conjunction of Venus and Sun in the first trade chart horoscope. The daily nearest chart in Figure 62 illustrates daily nearest coffee prices with Venus-Sun hard aspects overlaid along with a Venus retrograde event. Note how Coffee prices began to surge immediately as soon as the Venus Retrograde event of early 2014 concluded. This rally then peaked and stalled at a Venus-Sun hard aspect in April 2014.

Figure 62 Coffee futures and Venus

For 2015, Venus will make a 0 degree aspect to natal Sun from February 7 through February 11.

A 90 degree aspect will occur from April 23 through April 28.

A 180 degree aspect will occur from October 25 through October 30.

Venus will be Retrograde from July 24 through September 5.

The daily nearest chart in Figure 63 has been overlaid with various astro events involving Sun/natal Sun and Mars/natal Sun.

For 2015, Sun will make a 0 degree aspect to natal Sun from March 5 through March 11.

Sun will make a 90 degree aspect to natal Sun from June 5 through June 11.

Sun will make a 180 degree aspect to natal Sun from September 8 through

September 13.

Sun will make a 90 degree aspect to natal Sun from December 7 through December 11.
For 2015, Mars will make a 0 degree aspect to natal Sun from January 30 through February 7.

Mars will make a 90 degree hard aspect to natal Sun from June 2 through June 8.

Mars will make a 180 degree aspect to natal Sun from October 19 through October 25.

Mars will not exhibit any retrograde behavior in 2015.

It must also be noted that from October 25 through November 16, Jupiter will exhibit a 180 degree aspect to natal Sun.

Figure 63 Coffee futures and astro events

KCZ14 - Coffee - Daily Nearest OHLC Chart

Figure 64 Coffee futures and Mercury

Mercury has a bearing on Coffee price action as well. The daily nearest chart in Figure 64 has the Mercury 0,30,60,90,120 and 180 degree aspects to natal Sun overlaid on it. As well, Mercury Retrograde events are shown.

For 2015, Mercury will be Retrograde from:

January 22 through February 10
May 19 through June 11
September 18 through October 9

For 2015, Mercury will make a 0 degree aspect to natal Sun from March 22 through March 24.

Mercury will make 30 degree aspects to natal Sun from February 18 through February 20, March 2 through March 4, April 7 through April 9.

Mercury will make 60 degree aspects to natal Sun from April 22 through April 24 and December 20 through December 22.

Mercury will make 90 degree aspects to natal Sun from June 28 through July 1 and November 30 through December 2.

Mercury will make 120 degree aspects to natal Sun from July 16 through July 18 and November 11 through November 13.

Mercury will make a 180 degree aspect to natal Sun from August 17 through August 19.

Lastly, Coffee has a lunar influence. The chart in Figure 65 has New Moon events overlaid on it. Note how the New Moon at January 30, 2014 aligned to the start of an uptrend. The New Moon at April 28, 2014 marked the failure of an attempted rally. The trend on coffee prices changed markedly thereafter.

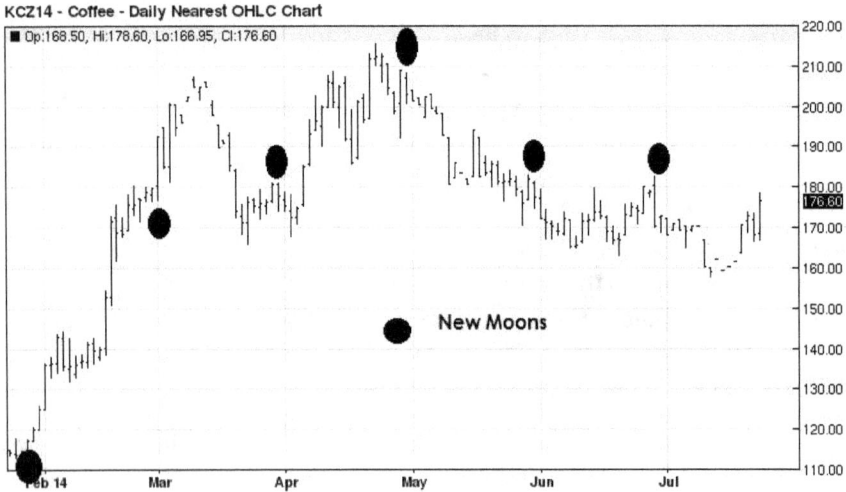

Figure 65 Coffee futures and New Moon events

For 2015, New Moon dates are January 5, February 3, March 5, April 4, May 4, June 2, July 2, July 31, August 29, September 28, October 27, November 25 and December 25.

5. ESOTERIC MATH TECHNIQUES

Gann Lines

Gann lines are a technique in which a starting point of a significant high or low is selected. From this point, angles (vectors) are projected outwards. These vectors are the 1x1, 1x2, 1x4, 1x8 and the 2x1, 4x1 and 8x1. The confusion with Gann lines comes from the scaling on the chart you are using. The chart you are using must be constructed so that the height and width of increments on the chart have equal dimensions. The portion of the chart shown in Figure 66 has been extracted from a larger chart made using the charting function in E*Trade. The width of a one month time frame on the chart was made to equal the dimension of a $20 price increment.

To illustrate the creation of Gann lines, I am going to use Gold as an example. On March 17, 2014, Gold made a price high at $1392. This is the point from which I wish to extend Gann lines.

Step 1: Take the $1392 and express it simply as the number 1392. Take the square root of the number 1392 and you get 37.3. This will be your time factor.

Step 2: Subtract 1 from 37.3 and re-square this figure to get 1318.

Step 3: We can now state that our time factor is 37.3 calendar days. We can further state that our price factor is 1392 minus 1318 = $74.

Step 4: From the March 17 date, you will extend a line so that the line passes through the time co-ordinate (March 17+37.3 days = April 23) and the price co-ordinate $1318. This line is the Gann 1x1 line.

Step 5: From the March 17 date, you will extend a line so that the line passes through the time co-ordinate (March 17+(37.3 x 2) days = May 30) and the price co-ordinate $1318. This line is the Gann 2x1 line.

Step 6: From the March 17 date, you will extend a line so that the line passes through the time co-ordinate (March 17+(0.5)*37.32)days = April 4) and the price co-ordinate $1318. This line is the Gann 1x2 line.

Step 7: From the March 17 date, you will extend a line so that the line passes through the time co-ordinate (March 17+(0.25)*37.32)days = March 26) and the price co-ordinate $1318. This line is the Gann 1x4 line.

The Gold price chart in Figure 66 has these Gann lines overlaid starting from the March $1392 high.

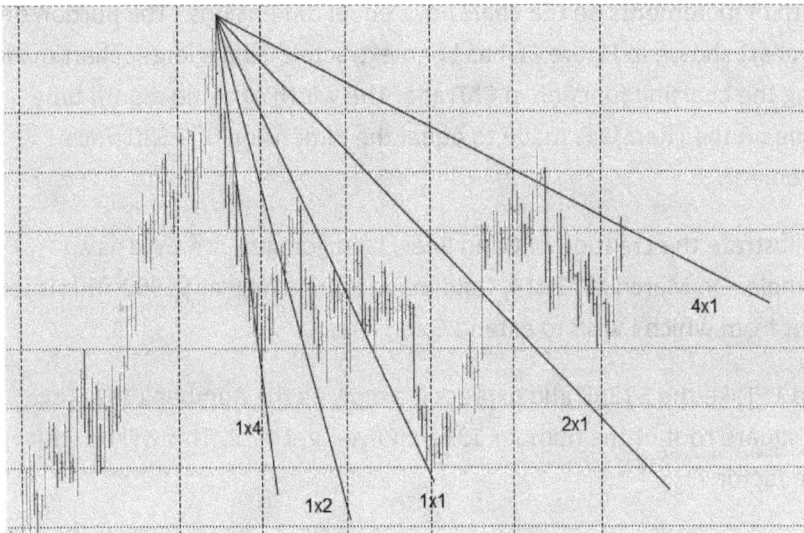

Figure 66 Gann Lines applied to a Gold Chart

Notice from the $1392 high, price action dropped, following the 1x4 line. A rally then pushed price up to the 1x1 line. The rally failed and price fell back to the 1x2 line. A sideways consolidation then ensued for several weeks. A significant low was registered at the 1x1 line. Price then rallied up through the 2x1 line and hit resistance at the 4x1 line. At this time of this chart was created in early August 2014, Gold price was struggling to get above the 4x1 line.

Harmonic Lines

In the early 1700s and scientist Sir Isaac Newton developed his theory of Universal Gravitation in which he said planets in our solar system are attracted to one another by gravity. Newton further said that space and time were absolute and that the world functioned according to an absolute order. Furthermore, he said that space was a three-dimensional entity and time was a two-dimensional entity.

In the early 1900's, Albert Einstein advanced his theory of Relativity that posited Newton's absolute model was outdated. Einstein said the passage of time of an object was related to its speed with respect to that of another observer. Thus was penned the concept of relative space- time in which space was not uniform.

Einstein further stated that relative space-time could be distorted depending on the density of matter. That is, space-time in the area of the Sun is more distorted because the Sun has a great, huge mass. Light particles travelling near the Sun are then distorted from their linear path due to the mass of the Sun.

Harmonic lines are based on this quantum theory. The whole notion of harmonic lines posits that the price of a stock, index or commodity can be thought of as a light particle or electron that can occupy different energy levels or orbital shells.

Author Fabio Oreste has done a masterful job of taking quantum physics, blending it with the curvature mathematics of Riemann and applying the whole thing to price charting. Price is considered to be akin to light particles. These light particles are then deflected by actions of planets. This deflection is what gives us price highs and lows on a chart. Oreste's book is entitled *Quantum Trading* and is available through Amazon.com. No trader's bookshelf should be without it.

The Oreste formula for harmonic calculation is :

Harmonic = (N x 360) + PSO ;

Where PSO = heliocentric planetary longitude x Conversion Scale
Where N= the harmonic level
Where Conversion Scale = 2^n ; 1,2,4,8,16 ....

When dealing with prices less than 360, the inverse variation of the formula is used.

Harmonic = (1/N x 360) + PSO

To go into a lengthy description of harmonics would quickly double the size of this manuscript. In the interest of brevity, what follows is a listing of the harmonic lines you may wish to overlay onto your various charts for 2015. You may be shocked to find how price action tends to closely respect these harmonics and sub-harmonics.

S&P500 Index

During 2015, consider drawing harmonic lines onto your daily chart of the S&P500 Index. Each line should start at January 1, 2015 and terminate at December 31, 2015.

Pluto Harmonics

January 1: 1723
December 31: 1725

January 1: 2083
December 31: 2085

Pluto sub-Harmonics

January 1: 1813
December 31: 1815

January 1: 1903
December 31: 1905

January 1: 1993
December 31: 1995

January 1: 2173
December 31: 2175

Neptune Harmonics

January 1: 1776.9
December 31: 1779.1

January 1: 2136.9
December 31: 2139.1

Neptune sub-Harmonics

January 1: 1866.9
December 31: 1869.1

January 1: 1956.9
December 31: 1959.1

January 1: 2046.9
December 31: 2049.1

January 1: 2226.9
December 31: 2229.1

Uranus Harmonics

January 1: 1815.41
December 31: 1819.34

January 1: 2175.41
December 31: 2179.34

January 1: 2535.41
December 31: 2539.34

Uranus sub-Harmonics

January 1: 1905.41
December 31: 1909.34

January 1: 1995.41
December 31: 1999.34

January 1: 2085.41
December 31: 2089.34

January 1: 2265.41
December 31: 2269.34

Saturn Harmonics

January 1: 1677.22
December 31: 1688.34

January 1: 2037.22
December 31: 2048.34

January 1: 2397.22
December 31: 2408.34

Saturn sub-Harmonics

January 1: 1767.22
December 31: 1778.34

January 1: 1857.22
December 31: 1868.34

January 1: 1947.22
December 31: 1958.34

January 1: 2127.22
December 31: 2138.34

January 1: 2217.22
December 31: 2228.34

January 1: 2307.22
December 31: 2318.34

Jupiter Harmonics

January 1: 1574.57
December 31: 1602.93

January 1: 1934.57
December 31: 1962.93

January 1: 2294.57
December 31: 2322.93

Jupiter sub-Harmonics

January 1: 1754.57
December 31: 1782.93

January 1: 1844.57
December 31: 1872.93

January 1: 2024.57
December 31: 2052.93

January 1: 2114.57
December 31: 2142.93

January 1: 2204.57
December 31: 2232.93

Nasdaq Index

During 2015, consider drawing harmonic lines onto your daily chart of the Nasdaq Index. Each line should start at January 1, 2015 and terminate at December 31, 2015.

Pluto Harmonics

January 1: 2573.0
December 31: 2580.76

January 1: 4013
December 31: 4020.76

January 1: 5453
December 31: 5460.76

Pluto sub-Harmonics

January 1: 3293
December 31: 3300.76

January 1: 3653
December 31: 3660.76

January 1: 4373
December 31: 4380.76

January 1: 4733
December 31: 4740.76

January 1: 5093
December 31: 5100.76

Neptune Harmonics

January 1: 2787.68
December 31: 2796.48

January 1: 4227.68
December 31: 4236.48

January 1: 5667.68
December 31: 5676.48

Neptune sub-Harmonics

January 1: 3507.68
December 31: 3516.48

January 1: 3867.68
December 31: 3876.48

January 1: 4587.68
December 31: 4596.48

January 1: 4947.68
December 31: 4956.48

January 1: 5307.68
December 31: 5316.48

Uranus Harmonics

January 1: 2941.64
December 31: 2957.36

January 1: 4381.64
December 31: 4397.36

January 1: 5821.64
December 31: 5837.36

Uranus sub-Harmonics

January 1: 3301.64
December 31: 3317.36

January 1: 3661.64
December 31: 3677.36

January 1: 4021.64
December 31: 4037.36

January 1: 4741.64
December 31: 4757.36

January 1: 5101.64
December 31: 5117.36

January 1: 5461.64
December 31: 5477.36

Saturn Harmonics

January 1: 3828.88
December 31: 3873.36

January 1: 5268.88
December 31: 5313.36

Saturn sub-Harmonics

January 1: 4188.88
December 31: 4233.36

January 1: 4548.88
December 31: 4593.36

January 1: 4908.88
December 31: 4953.36

January 1: 5628.88
December 31: 5673.36

Jupiter Harmonics

January 1: 3418.28
December 31: 3531.72

January 1: 4858.28
December 31: 4971.72

January 1: 6298.28
December 31: 6411.72

Jupiter sub-Harmonics

January 1: 3778.28
December 31: 3891.72

January 1: 4138.28
December 31: 4251.72

January 1: 4498.28
December 31: 4611.72

January 1: 5218.28
December 31: 5331.28

January 1: 5578.28
December 31: 5691.72

Dow Jones Industrial Average

During 2015, consider drawing harmonic lines onto your daily chart of the Dow Jones Industrial Average. Each line should start at January 1, 2015 and terminate at December 31, 2015.

Pluto Harmonics

January 1: 15533
December 31: 15540.76

January 1: 16973
December 31: 16980.76

January 1: 18413
December 31: 18420.76

Pluto sub-Harmonics

January 1: 15893
December 31: 15900.76

January 1: 16253
December 31: 16260.76

January 1: 16613
December 31: 16620.76

January 1: 17333
December 31: 17340.76

January 1: 17723
December 31: 17700.76

January 1: 18083
December 31: 18060.76

Neptune Harmonics

January 1: 15747.68
December 31: 15756.48

January 1: 17187.68
December 31: 17196.48

January 1: 18627.68
December 31: 18636.48

Neptune sub-Harmonics

January 1: 16107.68
December 31: 16116.48

January 1: 16467.68
December 31: 16476.48

January 1: 16827.68
December 31: 16836.48

January 1: 17547.68
December 31: 17556.48

January 1: 17907.68
December 31: 17916.48

January 1: 18267.68
December 31: 18276.48

Uranus Harmonics

January 1: 15885.92
December 31:

January 1: 15917.36
December 31:

January 1: 17325.92
December 31: 17357.36

January 1: 18765.92
December 31: 18797.36

Uranus sub-Harmonics

January 1: 16245.92
December 31: 16277.36

January 1: 16605.92
December 31: 16637.36

January 1: 16965.92
December 31: 16997.36

January 1: 17685.92
December 31: 17717.36

January 1: 18045.92
December 31: 18077.36

January 1: 18405.92
December 31: 18437.36

Saturn Harmonics

January 1: 15303.8
December 31: 15393.36

January 1: 16743.8
December 31: 16833.36

January 1: 18183.8
December 31: 18273.36

Saturn sub-Harmonics

January 1: 16023.8
December 31: 16113.36

January 1: 16383.8
December 31: 16473.36

January 1: 17103.8
December 31: 17193.36

January 1: 17463.8
December 31: 17553.36

January 1: 17823.8
December 31: 17913.36

Jupiter Harmonics

January 1: 14938.28
December 31: 15051.72

January 1: 16378.28
December 31: 16491.72

January 1: 17818.28
December 31: 17931.72

Jupiter sub-Harmonics

January 1: 15298.28
December 31: 15411.72

January 1: 15658.28
December 31: 15771.72

January 1: 16108.28
December 31: 16131.72

January 1: 16738.28
December 31: 16851.72

January 1: 17098.28
December 31: 17211.72

January 1: 17458.28
December 31: 17571.72

January 1: 18128.28
December 31: 18291.72

FTSE 100 Index

During 2015, consider drawing harmonic lines onto your daily chart of the FTSE 100 Index. Each line should start at January 1, 2015 and terminate at December 31, 2015.

Pluto Harmonics

January 1: 5606.5
December 31: 5610.38

January 1: 6326.5
December 31: 6330.38

January 1: 7046.5
December 31: 7050.38

Pluto sub-Harmonics

January 1: 5786.5
December 31: 5790.38

January 1: 5966.5
December 31: 5970.38

January 1: 6146.5
December 31: 6150.38

January 1: 6506.5
December 31: 6510.38

January 1: 6686.5
December 31: 6690.38

January 1: 6866.5
December 31: 6870.38

Neptune Harmonics

January 1: 5713.84
December 31: 5718.24

January 1: 6433.84
December 31: 6438.24

January 1: 7153.84
December 31: 7158.24

Neptune sub-Harmonics

January 1: 5893.84
December 31: 5898.24

January 1: 6073.84
December 31: 6078.24

January 1: 6253.84
December 31: 6258.24

January 1: 6613.84
December 31: 6618.24

January 1: 6793.84
December 31: 6798.24

January 1: 6973.84
December 31: 6978.24

Uranus Harmonics

January 1: 5790.82
December 31: 5798.68

January 1: 6510.82
December 31: 6518.68

January 1: 7230.82
December 31: 7238.68

Uranus sub-Harmonics

January 1: 5970.82
December 31: 5978.68

January 1: 6150.82
December 31: 6158.68

January 1: 6330.82
December 31: 6338.68

January 1: 6690.82
December 31: 6698.68

January 1: 6870.82
December 31: 6878.68

January 1: 7050.82
December 31: 7058.68

Saturn Harmonics

January 1: 5514.44
December 31: 5536.68

January 1: 6234.44
December 31: 6256.68

January 1: 6954.44
December 31: 6976.68

Saturn sub-Harmonics

January 1: 5694.44
December 31: 5716.68

January 1: 5874.44
December 31: 5896.68

January 1: 6054.44
December 31: 6076.68

January 1: 6414.44
December 31: 6436.68

January 1: 6594.44
December 31: 6616.68

January 1: 6774.44
December 31: 6796.68

January 1: 7134.44
December 31: 7156.68

Jupiter Harmonics

January 1: 5309.14
December 31: 5365.86

January 1: 6029.14
December 31: 6085.86

January 1: 6749.14
December 31: 6805.86

January 1: 7469.14
December 31: 7525.86

Jupiter sub-Harmonics

January 1: 5489.14
December 31: 5545.86

January 1: 5669.14
December 31: 5725.86

January 1: 5849.14
December 31: 5905.86

January 1: 6209.14
December 31: 6265.86

January 1: 6389.14
December 31: 6445.86

January 1: 6569.14
December 31: 6625.86

January 1: 6929.14
December 31:6985.86

January 1: 7109.14
December 31: 7165.86

January 1: 7289.14
December 31: 7345.86

German DAX Index

During 2015, consider drawing harmonic lines onto your daily chart of the DAX Index. Each line should start at January 1, 2015 and terminate at December 31, 2015.

Pluto Harmonics

January 1: 8333
December 31: 8340.76

January 1: 9773
December 31: 9780.76

January 1: 11213
December 31: 11220.76

Pluto sub-Harmonics

January 1: 8693
December 31: 8700.76

January 1: 9053
December 31: 9060.76

January 1: 9413
December 31: 9420.76

January 1: 10133
December 31: 10140.76

January 1: 10493
December 31: 10500.76

January 1: 10853
December 31: 10860.76

Neptune Harmonics

January 1: 8547.68
December 31: 8556.48

January 1: 9987.68
December 31: 9996.48

January 1: 11427.68
December 31: 11436.48

Neptune sub-Harmonics

January 1: 8907.68
December 31: 8916.48

January 1: 9267.68
December 31: 9276.48

January 1: 9627.68
December 31: 9636.48

January 1: 10347.68
December 31: 10356.48

January 1: 10707.68
December 31: 10716.48

January 1: 11067.68
December 31: 11076.48

Uranus Harmonics

January 1: 8701.64
December 31: 8717.36

January 1: 10141.64
December 31: 10157.36

January 1: 11581.64
December 31: 11597.36

Uranus sub-Harmonics

January 1: 9061.64
December 31: 9077.36

January 1: 9421.64
December 31: 9437.36

January 1: 9781.64
December 31: 9797.36

January 1: 10501.64
December 31: 10517.36

January 1: 10861.64
December 31: 10877.36

January 1: 11221.64
December 31: 11237.36

Saturn Harmonics

January 1: 8148.88
December 31: 8193.36

January 1: 9588.88
December 31: 9633.36

January 1: 11028.88
December 31: 11073.36

Saturn sub-Harmonics

January 1: 8508.88
December 31: 8553.36

January 1: 8668.88
December 31: 8913.36

January 1: 9228.88
December 31: 9273.36

January 1: 9948.88
December 31: 9993.36

January 1: 10308.88
December 31: 10353.36

January 1: 10668.88
December 31: 10713.36

January 1: 11388.88
December 31: 11433.36

Jupiter Harmonics

January 1: 7738.28
December 31:

January 1: 9178.28
December 31:

January 1: 10618.28
December 31:

Jupiter sub-Harmonics

January 1: 8458.28
December 31: 8571.72

January 1: 8818.28
December 31: 8931.72

January 1: 9538.28
December 31: 9651.72

January 1: 9898.28
December 31: 10011.72

January 1: 10258.28
December 31: 10371.72

January 1: 10978.28
December 31: 11091.72

January 1: 11388.28
December 31: 11451.72

Gold Futures

During 2015, consider drawing harmonic lines onto your daily chart of the Gold Futures. Each line should start at January 1, 2015 and terminate at December 31, 2015.

Pluto Harmonics

January 1: 1003.25
December 31: 1005.19

January 1: 1363.25
December 31: 1365.19

January 1: 1723.25
December 31: 1725.19

Pluto sub-Harmonics

January 1: 1093.25
December 31: 1095.19

January 1: 1183.25
December 31: 1185.19

January 1: 1273.25
December 31: 1275.19

January 1: 1453.25
December 31: 1455.19

January 1: 1543.25
December 31: 1545.19

January 1: 1633.25
December 31: 1635.19

January 1: 1813.25
December 31: 1815.19

January 1: 1903.25
December 31: 1905.19

Neptune Harmonics

January 1: 1056.92
December 31: 1059.12

January 1: 1416.92
December 31: 1419.12

January 1: 1776.92
December 31: 1779.12

Neptune sub-Harmonics

January 1: 1146.92
December 31: 1149.12

January 1: 1236.92
December 31: 1239.12

January 1: 1326.92
December 31: 1329.12

January 1: 1506.92
December 31: 1509.12

January 1: 1596.92
December 31: 1599.12

January 1: 1686.92
December 31: 1689.12

January 1: 1866.92
December 31: 1869.12

January 1: 1956.92
December 31: 1959.12

Uranus Harmonics

January 1: 1095.41
December 31: 1099.34

January 1: 1455.41
December 31: 1459.34

January 1: 1815.41
December 31: 1819.34

Uranus sub-Harmonics

January 1: 1185.41
December 31: 1189.34

January 1: 1275.41
December 31: 1279.34

January 1: 1365.41
December 31: 1369.34

January 1: 1545.41
December 31: 1549.34

January 1: 1635.41
December 31: 1639.34

January 1: 1725.41
December 31: 1729.34

January 1: 1905.41
December 31: 1909.34

Saturn Harmonics

January 1: 957.22
December 31: 968.34

January 1: 1317.22
December 31: 1328.34

January 1: 1677.22
December 31: 1688.34

Saturn sub-Harmonics

January 1: 1047.22
December 31: 1058.34

January 1: 1137.22
December 31: 1148.34

January 1: 1227.22
December 31: 1238.34

January 1: 1407.22
December 31: 1418.34

January 1: 1497.22
December 31: 1508.34

January 1: 1587.22
December 31: 1598.34

January 1: 1767.22
December 31: 1778.34

January 1: 1857.22
December 31: 1868.34

January 1: 1947.22
December 31: 1958.34

Jupiter Harmonics

January 1: 854.57
December 31: 882.93

January 1: 1214.57
December 31: 1242.93

January 1: 1574.57
December 31: 1602.93

January 1: 1934.57
December 31: 1962.93

Jupiter sub-Harmonics

January 1: 1034.57
December 31: 1062.93

January 1: 1124.57
December 31: 1152.93

January 1: 1304.57
December 31: 1332.93

January 1: 1394.57
December 31: 1422.93

January 1: 1484.57
December 31: 1512.93

January 1: 1664.57
December 31: 1692.93

January 1: 1754.57
December 31: 1782.93

January 1: 1844.57
December 31: 1872.93

Silver Futures

During 2015, consider drawing harmonic lines onto your daily chart of the Silver Futures. Each line should start at January 1, 2015 and terminate at December 31, 2015.

Pluto Harmonics

January 1: 10.04
December 31: 10.07

January 1: 20.08
December 31: 20.14
January 1: 40.17
December 31: 40.30

January 1: 80.34
December 31: 80.60

Pluto sub-Harmonics

January 1: 17.57
December 31: 17.60

January 1: 25.10
December 31: 25.17

January 1: 30.01
December 31: 30.20

January 1: 35.14
December 31: 35.23

January 1: 50.21
December 31: 50.37

Neptune Harmonics

January 1: 10.88
December 31: 10.91

January 1: 21.76
December 31: 21.83

January 1: 43.52
December 31: 43.66

Neptune sub-Harmonics
January 1: 16.32
December 31: 16.35

January 1: 19.04
December 31: 19.07

January 1: 27.20
December 31: 27.28

January 1: 32.64
December 31: 32.73

January 1: 38.08
December 31: 38.18

January 1: 54.40
December 31: 54.57

Uranus Harmonics

January 1: 11.73
December 31: 11.85

January 1: 23.45
December 31: 23.71

January 1: 46.91
December 31: 47.42

Uranus sub-Harmonics

January 1: 17.59
December 31: 17.77

January 1: 20.52
December 31: 20.73

January 1: 29.31
December 31: 29.63

January 1: 35.17
December 31: 35.55

January 1: 41.10
December 31: 41.47

January 1: 58.63
December 31: 59.27

Saturn Harmonics

January 1: 9.32
December 31: 9.50

January 1: 18.65
December 31: 19.00

January 1: 37.30
December 31: 38.00

January 1: 74.60
December 31: 76.00

Saturn sub-Harmonics

January 1: 16.31
December 31: 16.61

January 1: 23.31
December 31: 23.75

January 1: 27.97
December 31: 28.50

January 1: 32.63
December 31: 33.25

January 1: 46.62
December 31: 47.50

January 1: 55.94
December 31: 57.00

Jupiter Harmonics

January 1: 15.44
December 31: 16.33

January 1: 30.89
December 31: 32.66

January 1: 61.79
December 31: 65.33

Jupiter sub-Harmonics

January 1: 19.30
December 31: 20.41

January 1: 23.16
December 31: 24.49

January 1: 27.02
December 31: 28.57

January 1: 38.61
December 31: 40.82

January 1: 46.33
December 31: 48.98

January 1: 54.05
December 31: 57.58

Currency Futures (Canadian Dollar, Australian Dollar, Japanese Yen)

During 2015, consider drawing harmonic lines onto your daily chart of Canadian Dollar, Australian Dollar and Japanese Yen Currency futures. Each line should start at January 1, 2015 and terminate at December 31, 2015.

Pluto Harmonics

January 1: 0.6294
December 31: 0.6313

January 1: 1.2588
December 31: 1.2626

Pluto sub-Harmonics

January 1: 0.7868
December 31: 0.7891

January 1: 0.9442
December 31: 0.9469

January 1: 1.1016
December 31: 1.1047

Neptune Harmonics

January 1: 0.6830
December 31: 0.6852

January 1: 1.3661
December 31: 1.3705

Neptune sub-Harmonics

January 1: 0.8538
December 31: 0.8565

January 1: 1.0246
December 31: 1.0278

January 1: 1.1954
December 31: 1.1991

Uranus Harmonics

January 1: 0.7231
December 31: 0.7309

January 1: 1.4462
December 31: 1.4619

Uranus sub-Harmonics

January 1: 0.9039
December 31: 0.9137

January 1: 1.0847
December 31: 1.0965

January 1: 1.2655
December 31: 1.2793

Saturn Harmonics

January 1: 0.5833
December 31: 0.5944

January 1: 1.1667
December 31: 1.1889

Saturn sub-Harmonics

January 1: 0.7291
December 31: 0.7430

January 1: 0.8749
December 31: 0.8916

January 1: 1.0207
December 31: 1.0402

Jupiter Harmonics

January 1: 0.4807
December 31: 0.5090

January 1: 0.9614
December 31: 1.0181

January 1: 1.9228
December 31: 2.036

Jupiter sub-Harmonics

January 1: 0.6009
December 31: 0.6363

January 1: 0.7211
December 31: 0.7636

January 1: 0.8413
December 31: 0.8909

January 1: 0.8413
December 31: 0.8909

January 1: 1.2018
December 31: 1.2726

Currency Futures (Euro and British Pound)

During 2015, consider drawing harmonic lines onto your daily chart of Euro and British Pound Currency futures. Each line should start at January 1, 2015 and terminate at December 31, 2015.

Pluto Harmonics

January 1: 1.2696
December 31: 1.2735

Pluto sub-Harmonics

January 1: 1.5870
December 31: 1.5919

Neptune Harmonics

January 1: 1.3769
December 31: 1.3813

Neptune sub-Harmonics

January 1: 1.7212
December 31: 1.7267

Uranus Harmonics

January 1: 1.4678
December 31: 1.4836

Uranus sub-Harmonics

January 1: 1.8346
December 31: 1.8545

Saturn Harmonics

January 1: 1.1775
December 31: 1.1998

Saturn sub-Harmonics

January 1: 1.4719
December 31: 1.4998

January 1: 1.7663
December 31: 1.7998

Jupiter Harmonics

January 1: 0.9722
December 31: 1.0289

Jupiter sub-Harmonics

January 1: 1.2153
December 31: 1.2801

January 1: 1.4584
December 31: 1.5433

January 1: 1.7015
December 31: 1.8005

Wheat and Corn Futures

During 2015, consider drawing harmonic lines onto your daily chart of Wheat and Corn futures as you trade these contracts. Each line should start at January 1, 2015 and terminate at December 31, 2015.

Pluto Harmonics

January 1: 2.51
December 31: 2.51

January 1: 5.02
December 31: 5.03

January 1: 10.04
December 31: 10.07

Pluto sub-Harmonics

January 1: 3.13
December 31: 3.14

January 1: 3.76
December 31: 3.77

January 1: 4.39
December 31: 4.40

January 1: 6.27
December 31: 6.29

January 1: 7.53
December 31: 7.55

January 1: 8.78
December 31: 8.81

Neptune Harmonics

January 1: 2.72
December 31: 2.73

January 1: 5.44
December 31: 5.46

January 1: 10.89
December 31: 10.91

Neptune sub-Harmonics

January 1: 3.40
December 31: 3.41

January 1: 4.08
December 31: 4.09

January 1: 4.76
December 31: 4.77

January 1: 6.80
December 31: 6.82

January 1: 8.16
December 31: 8.18

January 1: 9.52
December 31: 9.54

Uranus Harmonics

January 1: 2.93
December 31: 2.96

January 1: 5.86
December 31: 5.92

January 1: 11.73
December 31: 11.85

Uranus sub-Harmonics

January 1: 3.66
December 31: 3.70

January 1: 4.39
December 31: 4.44

January 1: 5.12
December 31: 5.18

January 1: 7.32
December 31: 7.40

January 1: 8.78
December 31: 8.88

January 1: 10.24
December 31: 10.36

Saturn Harmonics

January 1: 2.33
December 31: 2.37

January 1: 4.66
December 31: 4.74

January 1: 9.32
December 31: 9.49

Saturn sub-Harmonics

January 1: 2.91
December 31: 2.96

January 1: 3.49
December 31: 3.55

January 1: 4.07
December 31: 4.14

January 1: 5.82
December 31: 5.92

January 1: 6.98
December 31: 7.10

January 1: 8.14
December 31: 8.28

Jupiter Harmonics

January 1: 1.93
December 31: 2.04

January 1: 3.86
December 31: 4.08

January 1: 7.72
December 31: 8.16

Jupiter sub-Harmonics

January 1: 2.41
December 31: 2.55

January 1: 2.89
December 31: 3.06

January 1: 3.37
December 31: 3.57

January 1: 4.82
December 31: 5.10

January 1: 5.79
December 31: 6.12

January 1: 6.75
December 31: 7.14

Soybean Futures

During 2015, consider drawing harmonic lines onto your daily chart of the S&P500 Index. Each line should start at January 1, 2015 and terminate at December 31, 2015.

Pluto Harmonics

January 1: 5.02
December 31: 5.03

January 1: 10.04
December 31: 10.07

Pluto sub-Harmonics

January 1: 7.52
December 31: 7.53

January 1: 8.77
December 31: 8.78

January 1: 12.55
December 31: 12.58

January 1: 15.06
December 31: 15.09

Neptune Harmonics

January 1: 5.44
December 31: 5.45

January 1: 10.88
December 31: 10.91

January 1: 21.76
December 31: 21.83

Neptune sub-Harmonics

January 1: 8.16
December 31: 8.17

January 1: 9.52
December 31: 9.53

January 1: 13.60
December 31: 13.63

January 1: 16.32
December 31: 16.35

Uranus Harmonics

January 1: 5.86
December 31: 5.92

January 1: 11.73
December 31: 11.85

January 1: 23.46
December 31: 23.70

Uranus sub-Harmonics

January 1: 7.32
December 31: 7.40

January 1: 8.78
December 31: 8.88

January 1: 10.24
December 31: 10.36

January 1: 14.66
December 31: 14.81

Saturn Harmonics

January 1: 4.66
December 31: 4.74

January 1: 9.32
December 31: 9.49

January 1: 18.65
December 31: 18.99

Saturn sub-Harmonics

January 1: 6.98
December 31: 7.10

January 1: 8.14
December 31: 8.28

January 1: 11.65
December 31: 11.86

January 1: 13.98
December 31: 14.23

January 1: 16.31
December 31: 16.60

Jupiter Harmonics

January 1: 7.72
December 31: 8.16

January 1: 15.44
December 31: 16.33

Jupiter sub-Harmonics

January 1: 9.65
December 31: 10.20

January 1: 11.58
December 31: 12.24

January 1: 13.51
December 31: 14.28

Crude Oil Futures

During 2015, consider drawing harmonic lines onto your daily chart of Crude Oil futures. Each line should start at January 1, 2015 and terminate at December 31, 2015.

Pluto Harmonics

January 1: 80.46
December 31: 80.70

January 1: 160.92
December 31: 161.41

Pluto sub-Harmonics

January 1: 100.57
December 31: 100.87

January 1: 120.68
December 31: 121.04

Neptune Harmonics

January 1: 43.59
December 31: 43.72

January 1: 87.18
December 31: 87.45

January 1: 174.36
December 31: 174.91

Neptune sub-Harmonics

January 1: 76.26
December 31: 76.51

January 1: 108.97
December 31: 109.31

Uranus Harmonics

January 1: 46.92
December 31: 47.42

January 1: 93.85
December 31: 94.84

January 1: 187.71
December 31: 189.48

Uranus sub-Harmonics

January 1: 70.38
December 31: 71.12

January 1: 82.11
December 31: 82.97

January 1: 117.31
December 31: 118.55

Saturn Harmonics

January 1: 74.69
December 31: 76.09

January 1: 149.39
December 31: 152.18

Saturn sub-Harmonics

January 1: 93.36
December 31: 95.11

January 1: 112.03
December 31: 114.13

January 1: 130.70
December 31: 133.15

Jupiter Harmonics

January 1: 61.84
December 31: 65.39

January 1: 123.69
December 31: 130.79

Jupiter sub-Harmonics

January 1: 77.30
December 31: 81.73

January 1: 92.76
December 31: 98.07

January 1: 108.22
December 31: 114.41

30 Year Bond Futures

During 2015, consider drawing harmonic lines onto your daily chart of
Bond futures. Each line should start at January 1, 2015 and terminate at
December 31, 2015.

Pluto Harmonics

January 1: 80.46
December 31: 80.70

January 1: 160.92
December 31: 161.41

Pluto sub-Harmonics

January 1: 120.68
December 31: 121.04

January 1: 140.79
December 31: 141.21

Neptune Harmonics

January 1: 87.18
December 31: 87.45

January 1: 174.36
December 31: 174.91

Neptune sub-Harmonics

January 1: 130.76
December 31: 131.13

January 1: 152.55
December 31: 153.03

Uranus Harmonics

January 1: 93.85
December 31: 94.84

January 1: 187.71
December 31: 189.48

Uranus sub-Harmonics

January 1: 117.31
December 31: 118.55

January 1: 140.77
December 31: 142.26

January 1: 164.23
December 31: 165.97

Saturn Harmonics

January 1: 74.69
December 31: 76.09

January 1: 149.39
December 31: 152.18

Saturn sub-Harmonics

January 1: 130.70
December 31: 133.15

Jupiter Harmonics

January 1: 123.69
December 31: 130.79

Jupiter sub-Harmonics

January 1: 154.61
December 31: 163.48

6. EPILOGUE

I have taken you on a wide ranging journey in this Almanac to acquaint you with the mathematical and astrological links between investor emotion and market behavior. I sincerely hope you will embrace Financial Astrology as a valuable tool to assist you in your trading and investing activity. I further hope you will pause often to reflect on the deeper connection between the financial markets, Astrology and the emotions of mankind.

On that note, I will leave you with the words of Neil Turok from his 2012 book, *The Universe Within*.

"Perseverance leads to enlightenment. And the truth is more beautiful than your wildest dreams".

7. GLOSSARY OF TERMS

Ascendant: One of four cardinal points on a horoscope, the Ascendant is situated in the East

Aspect: The angular relationship between two planets measured in degrees

Autumnal Equinox: (see Equinox) – That time of year when Sun is at 0 degrees Libra

Conjunct: An angular relationship of 0 degrees between two planets

Cosmo-biology: Changes in human emotion caused by changes in cosmic energy

Descendant: One of four cardinal points on a horoscope, the Descendant is situated in the West

Ephemeris: A daily tabular compilation of planetary and lunar positions

Equinox: An event occurring twice annually, an equinox event marks the time when the tilt of the Earth's axis is neither toward or away from the Sun

First Trade chart: A zodiac chart depicting the positions of the planets at the time a company's stock or a commodity future commenced trading on a recognized financial exchange

First Trade date: The date a stock or commodity futures contract first began trading on a recognized exchange

Full Moon: From a vantage point situated on Earth, when the Moon is seen to be 180 degrees to the Sun

Geocentric Astrology: That version of Astrology in which the vantage point for determining planetary aspects is the Earth

Heliocentric Astrology: That version of Astrology in which the vantage point for determining planetary aspects is the Sun

House: A 1/12th portion of the zodiac. Portions are not necessarily equal depending on the mathematical formula used to calculate the divisions

Lunar Eclipse: A lunar eclipse occurs when the Sun, Earth, and Moon are aligned exactly, or very closely so, with the Earth in the middle. The Earth blocks the Sun's rays from striking the Moon.

Lunar Month: (see Synodic Month)

Lunation: (see New Moon)

Mid-Heaven: One of four cardinal points on a horoscope, the Mid-Heaven is situated in the South

New Moon: From a vantage point situated on Earth, when the Moon is seen to be 0 degrees to the Sun

North Node of Moon: The intersection points between the Moon's plane and Earth's ecliptic are termed the North and South nodes. Astrologers tend to focus on the North node and Ephemeris tables clearly list the zodiacal position of the North Node for each calendar day

Orb: The amount of flexibility or tolerance given to an aspect

Retrograde motion: The apparent backwards motion of a planet through the zodiac signs when viewed from a vantage point on Earth

Sidereal Month: The Moon orbits Earth with a slightly elliptical pattern in approximately 27.3 days, relative to a fixed frame of reference.

Sidereal Orbital Period: The time required for a planet to make one full orbit of the Sun as viewed from a fixed vantage point on the Sun

Siderograph: A mathematical equation developed by astrologer Donald Bradley in 1946 (By plotting the output of the equation against date, inflection points can be seen on the plotted curve. It is at these inflection points that human emotion is most apt to change resulting in a trend change on the Dow Jones or S&P 500 Index)

Solar Eclipse: A solar eclipse occurs when the Moon passes between the Sun and Earth and fully or partially blocks the Sun.

Solstice: Occurring twice annually, a solstice event marks the time when the Sun reaches its highest or lowest altitude above the horizon at noon.

Synodic Month: During a sidereal month (see Sidereal Month), Earth will revolve part way around the Sun thus making the average apparent time between one New Moon and the next New Moon longer than the sidereal month at approximately 29.5 days. This 29.5 day time span is called a Synodic Month or sometimes a Lunar Month.

Synodic Orbital Period: The time required for a planet to make one full orbit of the Sun as viewed from a fixed vantage point on Earth

Vernal Equinox: That time of the year when Sun is at 0 degrees Aries.

Zodiac: An imaginary band encircling the 360 degrees of the planetary system divided into twelve equal portions of 30 degrees each

Zodiac Wheel: A circular image broken into 12 portions of 30 degrees each. Each portion represents a different astrological sign

8. OTHER BOOKS BY THE AUTHOR

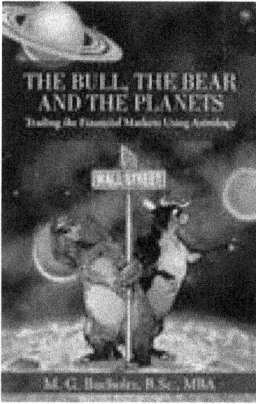

Once maligned by many, the subject of financial Astrology is now experiencing a revival as traders and investors seek deeper insight into the forces that move the financial markets.

The markets are a dynamic entity fueled by many factors, some of which we can easily comprehend, some of which are esoteric. This book introduces the reader to the notion that astrological phenomena can influence price action on financial markets and create trend changes across both short and longer term time horizons. From an introduction to the historical basics behind Astrology through to an examination of lunar Astrology and planetary aspects, the numerous illustrated examples in this book will introduce the reader the power of Astrology and its impact on both equity markets and commodity futures markets.

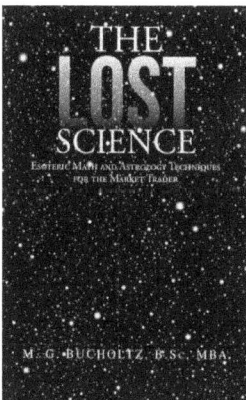

The financial markets are a reflection of the psychological emotions of traders and investors. These emotions ebb and flow in harmony with the forces of nature.

Scientific techniques and phenomena such as square root mathematics, the Golden Mean, the Golden Sequence, lunar events, planetary transits and planetary aspects have been used by civilizations dating as far back as the ancient Egyptians in order to comprehend the forces of nature.

The emotions of traders and investors can be seen to fluctuate in accordance with these forces of nature. Lunar events can be seen to align with trend changes on financial markets. Significant market cycles can be seen to align with planetary transits and aspects. Price patterns on stocks, commodity futures and market indices can be seen to conform to square root and Golden Mean mathematics.

In the early years of the 20th century the most successful traders on Wall Street, including the venerable W.D. Gann, used these scientific techniques and phenomena to profit from the markets. However, over the ensuing decades as technology has advanced, the science has been lost.

The Lost Science acquaints the reader with an extensive range of astrological and mathematical phenomena. From the Golden Mean and Fibonacci Sequence, to planetary transit lines and square roots through to an examination of lunar Astrology and planetary aspects, the numerous illustrated examples in this book will show the reader how these unique scientific phenomena impact the financial markets.

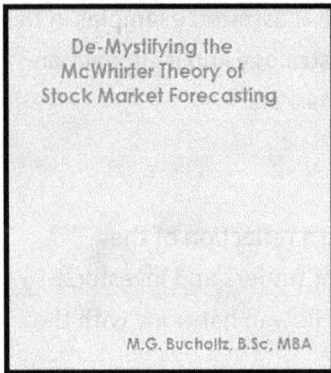

De-Mystifying the
McWhirter Theory of
Stock Market Forecasting

M.G. Bucholtz, B.Sc, MBA

Very little is known about Louise McWhirter, except that in 1937 she wrote the book *McWhirter Theory of Stock Market Forecasting.*

In my travels to places as far away as the British Library in London, England to research financial Astrology, not once did I come across any other books by her. Not once did I find any other book from her era that even mentioned her name. All of this I find to be deeply mysterious.

I am almost of the opinion that the name Louise McWhirter may have been a *nom de plume,* or as we say in English – *a pen name* for a writer seeking to conceal his or her identity – and for good reason. In the early decades of the 20th century many American States had arcane laws that can be traced back to the days of the Salem Witch Trials. These statute laws prohibited the commercial use of occult science. That is, you could not openly set up a shop to conduct tarot card readings or perform palm reading analyses. And using Astrology to predict the stock market – well, that too would have been illegal.

Despite these laws, the early decades of the 20th century saw many successful traders on Wall Street use Astrology as a tool to gauge the markets. The underlying premise of their efforts was that events in our cosmos influence our emotions. These changing emotions then impact our buying and selling decisions which make stock prices and market indices rise and fall. Chief among the many traders who used Astrology was the respected W.D. Gann. I suspect that one of these traders, (perhaps even Gann himself) seeking to write a book documenting his Astrology methodology for the benefit of future generations, concocted the *pen name* Louise McWhirter as the author for his book. But, no matter who wrote *McWhirter Theory of Stock Market Forecasting*, the methodology outlined in it was accurate in the late 1930s when it was written and it remains accurate today. The trader or investor having a comfortable grasp on this methodology will enjoy a distinct advantage over those traders and investors who are unwilling to make the connection between human emotion and stock market price movements.

ABOUT THE AUTHOR

Malcolm Bucholtz, B.Sc, MBA is a graduate of Queen's University Faculty of Engineering in Canada and Heriot Watt University in Scotland where he received an MBA degree. After working in Canadian industry for far too many years, Malcolm followed his passion for the financial markets by becoming an Investment Advisor/Commodity Trading Advisor with an independent brokerage firm in western Canada. Today, he resides in western Canada where he trades the financial markets using technical chart analysis, esoteric mathematics and the astrological principles outlined in this book.

Malcolm is the author of two books. His first book, The Bull, the Bear and the Planets, offers the reader an introduction to Financial Astrology and makes the case that there are esoteric and astrological phenomena that influence the financial markets. His second book, The Lost Science, takes the reader on a deeper journey into planetary events and unique mathematical phenomena that influence financial markets.

Malcolm maintains both a website (www.investingsuccess.ca) and a blog (www.astrologicaltrading.wordpress.com) where he provides traders and investors with astrological insights into the financial markets. He also offers a monthly **Astrology E-Alert** service where subscribers receive a weekly preview of pending astrological events that stand to influence markets.